WHO KNOWS WHAT IS GOOD?

A Commentary on the Books of

Proverbs and Ecclesiastes

KATHLEEN A. FARMER

WM. B. EERDMANS PUBLISHING CO., GRAND RAPIDS

THE HANDSEL PRESS LTD, EDINBURGH

Copyright © 1991 by William B. Eerdmans Publishing Company
First published 1991 by William B. Eerdmans Publishing Company
255 Jefferson Ave. S.E., Grand Rapids, Michigan 49503
and
The Handsel Press Limited
139 Leith Walk, Edinburgh EH6 8NS

Reprinted 1996

Library of Congress Cataloging-in-Publication Data

Farmer, Kathleen Anne.
Who knows what is good?: a commentary on the books of Proberbs
and Ecclesiastes / Kathleen A. Farmer
p.   cm.   — (International theological commentary)
Includes bibliographical references and index.
ISBN 0 – 8028 0161 – 7 (pbk.)
1. Bible. O.T. Proberbs — Commentaries.   2. Bible. O.T. Ecclesiastes —
Commentaries.   I. Title.   II. Series.
BS1465.3.F37   1991
223'.707 — dc20   90 – 48075
                                                            CIP

Handsel Press ISBN 0 871828 08 2

Dedicated with gratitude to W. J. A. Power,
Professor of Old Testament at Perkins School of Theology,
who first introduced me to "the Words of the Wise,"
and to my students at United Theological Seminary,
who continue to instruct me in Wisdom's ways.

CONTENTS

ABBREVIATIONS

ANET   *Ancient Near Eastern Texts,* ed. James B. Pritchard
JB   Jerusalem Bible
KJV   King James (or Authorized) Version
LXX   Septuagint
MT   Masoretic Text
NAB   New American Bible
NEB   New English Bible
NIV   New International Version
NJV   New Jewish Version (Jewish Publication Society, 1985)
RSV   Revised Standard Version
TEV   Today's English Version

EDITORS' PREFACE

The Old Testament alive in the Church: this is the goal of the *International Theological Commentary.* Arising out of changing, unsettled times, this Scripture speaks with an authentic voice to our own troubled world. It witnesses to God's ongoing purpose and to his caring presence in the universe without ignoring those experiences of life that cause one to question his existence and love. This commentary series is written by front-rank scholars who treasure the life of faith.

Addressed to ministers and Christian educators, the *International Theological Commentary* moves beyond the usual critical-historical approach to the Bible and offers a *theological* interpretation of the Hebrew text. Thus, engaging larger textual units of the biblical writings, the authors of these volumes assist the reader in the appreciation of the theology underlying the text as well as its place in the thought of the Hebrew Scriptures. But more, since the Bible is the book of the believing community, its text has acquired ever more meaning through an ongoing interpretation. This growth of interpretation may be found both within the Bible itself and in the continuing scholarship of the Church.

Contributors to the *International Theological Commentary* are Christians—persons who affirm the witness of the New Testament concerning Jesus Christ. For Christians, the Bible is *one* scripture containing the Old and New Testaments. For this reason, a commentary on the Old Testament may not ignore the second part of the canon, namely, the New Testament.

Since its beginning, the Church has recognized a special relationship between the two Testaments. But the precise character of this bond has been difficult to define. Thousands of books and articles have discussed the issue. The diversity of views represented in these publications makes us aware that the Church is not of one mind in expressing the "how" of this relationship. The authors of this commentary share a developing consensus that any serious explanation of the Old Testament's relationship to the New will uphold the integrity of the Old Testament. Even though Christianity is rooted in the soil of the Hebrew Scriptures, the biblical interpreter must take care lest he "christianize" these Scriptures.

Authors writing in this commentary will, no doubt, hold varied views concerning *how* the Old Testament relates to the New. No attempt has been made to dictate one viewpoint in this matter. With the whole Church, we are convinced that the relationship between the two Testaments is real and substantial. But we recognize also the diversity of opinions among Christian scholars when they attempt to articulate fully the nature of this relationship.

In addition to the Christian Church, there exists another people for whom the Old Testament is important, namely, the Jewish community. Both Jews and Christians claim the Hebrew Bible as Scripture. Jews believe that the basic teachings of this Scripture point toward and are developed by the Talmud, which assumed its present form about 500 C.E. On the other hand, Christians hold that the Old Testament finds its fulfillment in the New Testament. The Hebrew Bible, therefore, belongs to both the Church and the Synagogue.

Recent studies have demonstrated how profoundly early Christianity reflects a Jewish character. This fact is not surprising because the Christian movement arose out of the context of first-century Judaism. Further, Jesus himself was Jewish, as were the first Christians. It is to be expected, therefore, that Jewish and Christian interpretations of the Hebrew Bible will reveal similarities *and* disparities. Such is the case. The authors of the *International Theological Commentary* will refer to the various Jewish traditions that they consider important for an appreciation of the Old Testament text. Such references will enrich our understanding of certain biblical passages and, as an extra gift, offer us insight into the relationship of Judaism to early Christianity.

An important second aspect of the present series is its *international* character. In the past, Western church leaders were considered to be *the* leaders of the Church—at least by those living in the West! The theology and biblical exegesis done by these scholars dominated the thinking of the Church. Most commentaries were produced in the Western world and reflected the lifestyle, needs, and thoughts of its civilization. But the Christian Church is a worldwide community. People who belong to this universal Church reflect differing thoughts, needs, and lifestyles.

Today the fastest growing churches in the world are to be found, not in the West, but in Africa, Indonesia, South America, Korea, Taiwan, and elsewhere. By the end of this century, Christians in these areas will outnumber those who live in the West. In our age, especially, a commentary on the Bible must transcend the parochialism of Western civilization and be sensitive to issues that are the special problems of persons who live outside of the "Christian" West, issues such as race relations, personal survival and fulfillment, liberation, revolution, famine, tyranny, disease, war, the poor, religion and state. Inspired of God, the authors of the Old Testament knew what life is like on the edge of existence. They addressed themselves to everyday people who often faced more than everyday problems. Refusing to limit God to the "spiritual," they portrayed him as one who heard and knew the cries of people in pain (see Exod. 3:7-8). The contributors to the *International Theological Commentary* are persons who prize the writings of these biblical authors as a word of life to our world today. They read the Hebrew Scriptures in the twin contexts of ancient Israel and our modern day.

The scholars selected as contributors underscore the international aspect of the series. Representing very different geographical, ideological, and ecclesiastical backgrounds, they come from over seventeen countries. Besides scholars from such traditional countries as England, Scotland, France, Italy, Switzerland, Canada, New Zealand, Australia, South Africa, and the United States, contributors from the following places are included: Israel, Indonesia, India, Thailand, Singapore, Taiwan, and countries of Eastern Europe. Such diversity makes for richness of thought. Christian scholars living in Buddhist, Muslim, or Socialist lands may be able to offer the World Church insights into the biblical message—insights to which the scholarship of the West could be blind.

The proclamation of the biblical message is the focal concern of the *International Theological Commentary*. Generally speaking, the authors of these commentaries value the historical-critical studies of past scholars, but they are convinced that these studies by themselves are not enough. The Bible is more than an object of critical study; it is the revelation of God. In the written Word, God has disclosed himself and his will to humankind. Our authors see themselves as servants of the Word which, when rightly received, brings *shalom* to both the individual and the community.

George A. F. Knight
Fredrick Carlson Holmgren

PROLOGUE

What is wisdom? How can one be wise in the world today? Does wisdom somehow stand in opposition to "faith?"

I once overheard a conversation between two small children who were sitting in the back seat of my car on the way home from church.

"Fasten your seat belt," said the first child.

"Why should I?" demanded the second. "The pastor said if I trust in the LORD, the LORD will take care of me."

"Well!" came the first child's indignant reply, "You can't expect God to do everything for you!"

The questions raised by these children parallel those raised by the body of OT writings we call "wisdom literature." What is the nature of faith and how does one go about living out one's life in a faithful way? Is it necessary to choose between trusting in the LORD and taking basic precautions for safety in a hazardous world? The issues are as alive for us today as they were for the original audiences addressed by Proverbs and Ecclesiastes.

"Who knows what is good?" asks the speaker in Eccl. 6:12. How shall we live out our brief lives "under the sun?" Can the "teaching of the wise" and the "fear of the LORD" be equally appropriate ways to achieve "life" in its God-intended abundance? (Compare Prov. 13:14 with Prov. 14:27). These are the issues addressed by the two "companion volumes" which are found side by side in most modern versions of the Bible. Taken together, Proverbs and Ecclesiastes represent the variety of answers which our ancestors in the faith have given and which we ourselves may still give to such questions.

This commentary will assume that the preservation of such diversity of opinion was a deliberate and inspired decision on the part of the faithful who handed these materials down to us. Such

1

differences were included for our edification. It would be theologically presumptuous of us to ignore them or to deny their existence in the text. The unity which holds the two books together and which ties them into the heart of our canon of Scripture is not a unity of opinion but a unity of attitude: a willingness on the part of their composers to undertake a search for answers without giving up either their reasoning abilities or their faith.

INTRODUCTION TO THE
WORDS OF THE WISE

Proverbs begins and Ecclesiastes ends with advice on how to read what these books contain: those who study the "words of the wise" should *begin* with the fear of the LORD (Prov. 1:7) and *end* with the keeping of God's commandments (Eccl. 12:13). The phrase "words of the wise" *(dibrey hakamim)* occurs only four times in the Hebrew Bible, and all four occurrences are in Proverbs and Ecclesiastes. The term seems to indicate a particular body or collection of material, perhaps limited to the contents of these two books alone. We do not know whether or not "wise" in this phrase refers to a particular class of people with special education or training. In many places in the OT "wise" refers to those who are clever or show physical as well as mental agility. In some cases the term "wise" may have been used simply to designate those whose sayings demonstrated unusual insight or depth. However, the material in our present-day versions of Proverbs and Ecclesiastes seems more like the product of studied reflection, expressed in more poetic and articulate fashion than the short, pithy commentary we usually think of as "folk wisdom" or folk proverbs.

The Hebrew word for "wise" in this phrase is plural, indicating that more than one wise person has contributed to the material to which the term refers. Although the book of Proverbs begins with the heading "The Proverbs of Solomon," the biblical text itself attributes the final chapters of the book to other sources (Prov. 30:1 and 31:1). Both men and women could be counted among the "wise" in Israel, as 2 Sam. 14:2-20 and 2 Sam. 20:16-22 indicate, and Prov. 31:1 openly states that the text which follows contains the "words of Lemuel king of Massa, which his mother taught him." It is also quite possible that later contributors or collectors added comments or observations to the body of material

3

as a whole. (The final chapter of the book of Ecclesiastes clearly contains comments about, rather than by, the "Preacher.") The traditional understanding that Solomon had some role in formulating both Proverbs and Ecclesiastes may be another way of affirming the need to hold both books together as the two essential facets of "wisdom."

Whether the opening and closing bits of advice on how to read Proverbs and Ecclesiastes originated with the wise ones themselves, or whether they reflect the opinions of those who collected, arranged, and handed these words down to us in the form in which we have received them, it is clear that this counsel has now become a part of our canon of Scripture. As such, it warns us that the "words of the wise" must be seen in their proper context. They cannot be rightly understood apart from the rest of the faith traditions of Israel.

THE ORDER OF ARRANGEMENT

Modern Hebrew Bibles separate Proverbs from Ecclesiastes (following a tradition begun in the 15th or 16th cent. C.E.) in order to group the five "festival scrolls" (Ruth, Song of Songs, Ecclesiastes, Lamentations, and Esther) together as a convenient unit. However, all of the oldest witnesses to the arrangement of the books in the biblical canon list Proverbs and Ecclesiastes next to each other, and in that order. Most modern English translations follow the older tradition.

This commentary will assume that our ancestors in the faith intended for us to read Proverbs and Ecclesiastes together, as a collection with a "prologue" (Prov. 1:2-7) and an "epilogue" (Eccl. 12:11-14). In the following pages, the assumption will consistently be made that each book should be read in the light of the other, and that both should be interpreted in light of their present context within the whole canon of our faith. This is a position which has been defended quite well by Gerald H. Wilson ("'The Words of the Wise,'" 175-192).

HARMONY OR COUNTERPOINT?

Readers who go to the biblical texts expecting every book (or every verse) to give them unambiguous advice on how to think and act in a faithful manner are often puzzled or disturbed by what they find within the books of Ecclesiastes and Proverbs. The wise ones whose words have been preserved for us in Proverbs and Ecclesiastes were primarily concerned with the question of goodness. What *is* good for humankind? What should humans do with or in their lives on earth? But the answers given by the wise who contributed to these two volumes were not all the same. Consider for example the question of the degree to which human beings can expect justice or retribution from God. A quick comparison of such passages as Prov. 2:21-22 or 3:9-10 with Eccl. 8:14 or 9:11 indicates the radical differences of opinion preserved in the "words of the wise."

Modern Western interpreters often find this lack of unanimity disturbing. Critics often have felt the need to offer explanations to account for the variety of opinion they have perceived within and between these two books.

Some scholars assume that the book of Proverbs represents the "norm" in Israelite wisdom thinking and that Ecclesiastes contains the opinions of one who protests or objects to that "norm." (James L. Crenshaw, *Old Testament Wisdom*, promotes this viewpoint.) Others account for the differences of opinion expressed in these books by theorizing different settings for their composition. Those who spoke to a stable, settled, and orderly society might make observations about reality that would not hold true for those who lived in troubled or chaotic times. (See Frank Crüsemann, "The Unchangeable World: The 'Crisis of Wisdom' in Koheleth.") Many scholars have argued that the original words of the wise were secular (non-religious) observations which were later amended by pious editors whose comments served to modify the original texts. (See George Barton, *Ecclesiastes*.) It is possible, however, that the lack of unanimity which troubles modern critics was not a problem for our ancestors. It is quite likely that modern Western literature has conditioned modern readers to expect a certain type of consistency (lack of internal self-contradiction) that was not expected by ancient readers.

I suggest that the literary conventions of Israel were quite different from our own, that those who collected the "words of the wise" and those who found them worthy of inclusion in our canon of Scripture were not as concerned with unanimity or consistency as we often are. Studying the texts themselves leads to the conclu-

5

sion that plurality of thought was not merely tolerated but was actually embraced and celebrated by the wise and by those who held them in esteem. We modern readers ought not to expect the biblical writings to conform to our own literary notions of propriety. It would be more accurate to think of the disagreements we find within the "words of the wise" as ideas in "counterpoint" or in "creative conflict" with each other (Derek Kidner, *The Wisdom of Proverbs, Job, and Ecclesiastes,* 116).

It is my assumption that those who finalized the canon wanted this variety of opinion to coexist and to be preserved as a part of our faith tradition. The wise men and women of Israel and those who handed their wisdom down to us apparently agreed that diversity was a part of wisdom, that ideas did not collide in space, and that different solutions might be needed at different times for the pressing problems which always have and always will confront the faithful.

Thus, I plan to proceed under the assumption that it is the final form of the canon which constitutes the inspired tradition. As the speaker in Ecclesiastes says, "Better is the end of a thing than its beginning" (Eccl. 7:8). Whether or not the statements of piety now found in Proverbs and Ecclesiastes were added on at a later date, the fact is that they now stand in a position to reframe our understanding of the whole collection. We ought to take our clues from those who handed the material down to us in this form and remember as we read the text that the fear of the LORD is both the beginning, the end, and the filter through which all of the other words of the wise should be examined. At the same time we should insist, as our ancestors in the faith consistently have done, that all of the individual parts of the wisdom tradition should be read in light of the whole body of sacred writings we call Scripture.

ISRAEL AMONG THE NATIONS

Readers who pay close attention to Israel's own memories concerning its origins are not surprised when scholars uncover evidence that the people of Israel shared certain customs, worldviews, and forms of expression with their neighbors in the ancient Near East. Israel clearly understood itself to have close cultural and family ties with the peoples of Mesopotamia and Egypt. Abraham's ancestry is traced to Mesopotamia, and his closest relatives are said to have remained there. His firstborn son had an Egyptian mother and wife, Moses was said to have been raised in an Egyptian pharaoh's court and to have married a "Cushite" woman, and so forth (Gen. 11, 21, 24, 28; Exod. 2; Num. 12; Deut. 26:5). The sages of Israel were also conscious of (and probably were familiar with) other wisdom traditions from neighboring countries (1 Kgs. 4:30-31). It is even possible, as some scholars argue, that "the Book of Proverbs—and especially its second collection [chs. 10–22]—served as learning material" in schools that "were inspired by an Egyptian archetype" (Nil Shupak, "The 'Sitz im Leben' of the Book of Proverbs," 117).

Egyptian wisdom compilations frequently have general elements of form and content similar to those found in parts of Proverbs. But in at least one case, it is possible to say that some literary dependence is evident: The Instruction of Amenemope (also spelled Amen-em-opet or Amenophis) and Prov. 22:17–24:22 coincide in more ways than can be reasonably attributed to chance. When such striking similarities are found between the sayings of the wise in Israel and in other lands, the question of "who did the borrowing?" is frequently raised. Few scholars would deny that there is more than a casual relationship between these two collections. There is, however, a great deal of debate over the specific nature of that relationship.

Andrew K. Helmbold's review of scholarly opinions regarding the relationship between the Instruction of Amenemope and Prov. 22:17–24:22 indicates the degree to which answers to such questions can differ ("The Relationship of Proverbs and Amenemope," 348-359). I would argue, however, that such questions as whether or not a particular saying is indigenous to Israel are irrelevant to our present task. Even if a particular saying in Proverbs could be shown to have been borrowed from another land, the fact that it lived on in its new environment seems to me to indicate that it struck a responsive chord or served a useful function in its adoptive "home." The comparison of texts does, however, bring us to the realization that the wise women and men of Israel did not live, speak, or write in a cultural vacuum.

Many wisdom texts from other cultures have been discovered and translated over the past century. Each could be said to contribute to our understanding of the wider contexts in which the sages of Israel lived and worked. However, in this commentary only a few specific

7

texts from other cultures will be mentioned. References will be limited to those writings which either bear a particularly close resemblance to parts of Proverbs and Ecclesiastes or which may give us specific insights into the cultural and historical settings and assumptions of the authors of the biblical texts. Thus, for example, the Aramaic text known as the Words of Ahiqar and several of the Egyptian instructions will be mentioned in an attempt to understand the cultural assumptions of Prov. 13:24 and 23:13-14.

The Words of Ahiqar is a 5th-cent. B.C.E. collection of wisdom sayings found on Elephantine (a narrow island in the Nile, located near the present-day site of the Aswan Dam). In the second half of the 5th cent. a small colony of Jewish men and women lived on Elephantine, which apparently served as a frontier outpost for mercenary soldiers serving the Persian king. Although the Ahiqar texts were found in the same location as letters and legal documents originating from the Jewish colony, the Words of Ahiqar do not appear to be Jewish in origin. The story which acts as a setting for the sayings describes Ahiqar as a "wise scribe" in the courts of the Assyrian kings Sennacherib and Esarhaddon (who ruled at the end of the 8th and the beginning of the 7th cents.), and the sayings themselves refer to the deity Shamash (the sun-god, worshipped by the Assyrians as well as by other Semitic peoples). However, Ahiqar is also mentioned in the apocryphal book of Tobit, which probably indicates that his story was known and referred to by Jews in other communities as well as being known to the Jews of Elephantine. Thus, Ahiqar's assumptions and opinions concerning what is "wise" can contribute to our understanding of what Israel's wisdom shares (or does not share) with its Near Eastern counterparts.

Readers who wish to dig more deeply into the relationship between the wisdom of Israel and the wisdom of other ancient Near Eastern cultures will find an extensive review of the subject in William McKane, *Proverbs,* 51-208. Non-specialists will find English translations of the non-Israelite texts mentioned in the body of this commentary in James B. Pritchard, *Ancient Near Eastern Texts* (abbreviated as *ANET*).

THE "WORDS OF THE WISE" AND FEMINIST CONCERNS

Those who wish to use the wisdom texts for guidance in their own lives must learn to distinguish between the attitude the "wise" in

Israel had towards women (to whatever limited extent it is possible to discover such information) and what implications that attitude has for us today. Several factors complicate modern attempts to discover what the "wise" really thought about having women involved in the wisdom enterprise. First of all, the evidence is ambiguous. We can see, on the one hand, that at least one woman actually is named as the source of a section of the book of Proverbs (Prov. 31:1). This section of the book also contains an idealistic portrait of a strong and capable woman who both manages a large household with ease and engages in a number of financial and business endeavors. The frequent use of "I" (the first person singular, which has no gender designation) in the first nine chapters of Proverbs also leaves open the possibility that some of the wisdom teachers who contributed to that section were female.

On the other hand, we cannot ignore the fact that the "wise" consistently addressed their sayings to "sons" rather than to "daughters." The masculine plural can mean "children" (both male and female children), but the semantic range of the frequently used singular ("son") does not seem to include the possibility that the person addressed is female. And the shorter ("Solomonic") sayings sections in Proverbs which speak disparagingly (in at least a half dozen verses) of nagging or contentious wives never mention husbands who manifest similar characteristics.

Furthermore, it is inevitable that those who read the texts in translation will be influenced by the unexamined cultural assumptions of the translators. Translations can skew the reader's conclusions concerning the attitude of the wise toward women. For instance, it is clearly the case that both poles of human behavior (wisdom and folly) are personified in Prov. 1–9 as females who call out to the "simple" to entice them. Both the magnificent portrait of Wisdom in 8:4-36 and the degrading picture of Temptation in 7:6-23 are presented to us as though they were women. However, in spite of this balancing of poles, English-speaking audiences often receive overwhelmingly negative impressions from the passages which portray temptation in a feminine guise. This is due as much to the biases of modern translators as it is to the patriarchal nature of OT societies. An easily seen example is the rendering of a Hebrew term meaning "another man's wife" as "adulteress" in the RSV of 6:26. When the young man is advised (in Hebrew) to stay away from another man's wife, several English translations (including RSV, NIV, and KJV) change the advice into a warning to avoid the *adulteress*. In a similar way, the RSV translation of "loose woman" and "adventuress" for terms with the literal sense of a "stranger" or a "foreigner" (in 2:16) turns what is basically xenophobia into what seems to be misogyny. (See the Commentary on these sections.)

Suppose, however, that we could discover (with some degree of accuracy) what the wisdom teachers in Israel (as individuals or as a group) thought about women. What conclusions could we draw from such information? How might we apply this information in our own life settings? In my opinion those who want to find guidance for living out their own lives in accordance with God's intentions must first learn to distinguish between the prescriptive and the descriptive intentions of various portions of Scripture. Sometimes we do this automatically, without conscious thought or effort. For instance, when we hear that Abraham and Sarah had slaves, we do not automatically conclude that we ourselves should own slaves or support the practice of slavery. Rather, we assume that the texts mention slavery descriptively: they *describe* how things were in Sarah and Abraham's time. Most of us realize that we ought not to understand the patriarchal stories prescriptively, that is, that we ought not to assume that the way things *were* in ancient times is necessarily the way things *ought to be* or the way *God wants* them to be in our time. We realize that those whom God chose to become instruments of blessing in the world lived in socially and historically limited settings.

In a similar way we ought to recognize the descriptive nature of Qohelet's apparently negative statement in Eccl. 7:28. According to many interpreters, Qohelet claims that he has not found one trustworthy woman among a thousand (the meaning of the Hebrew text is unclear at this point). But, his lamentable experience (even if true) is not meant to be prescriptively understood: it ought not to be generalized or universalized. It is not a statement of what is true everywhere or for all time.

As we read the "words of the wise" we need to remind ourselves that in the world in which the biblical traditions originated (and in which they were preserved and handed down), most of the social, economic, and political power was wielded by men. Most of the prophets, the historians, the scribes, and probably most of the sages were men. It would only be natural to expect that in such a world most of the stories told—and most of the proverbs or wisdom sayings preserved—would represent the male (in that society's) point of view. From that perspective we might conclude that it is rather surprising that we find as many positive portrayals of women as we do.

Once again I suggest that the many problematic texts must be read in light of their present literary context. Women *may have been* a neglected element in the original audiences addressed by the "wise" in Israel (although this is by no means a foregone conclusion). But once the "words of the wise" are incorporated into the rest of biblical story, once they become a part of the whole canon of Scripture, they have to be understood in a new way. Taken as a whole, the Scriptures proclaim the value and validity of female as well as of male aspects of human experience. Taken as a whole, our canon of faith upholds the dignity, the value, and the worth of every human being. Since the canonical texts proclaim that the powerless, the devalued, and the disenfranchised are the heirs of the promise, then we who read Proverbs and Ecclesiastes ought to understand the imbalances they contain as indicative of the way things *were* in a given historical setting, rather than as the way things *ought* to be or as the way God would like them to be.

My reading of the whole canon of Scripture has convinced me that the Word of God is addressed to male and female human beings alike. The God who communicates with us through the biblical texts created both women and men to act as God's images in the world, and this God wants women and men to work in equal partnership with each other in order to carry out God's purposes in the world.

A close reading of the biblical texts makes it clear that the human societies in which the biblical witnesses lived did not always share this understanding of God's intentions. Those who handed down the traditions of our faith, those who collected them and preserved them in the forms in which we now find them, and those who have translated them into languages other than Hebrew have not always recognized God's advocacy of the full humanity of both women and men. Nevertheless, we ought to insist on the legitimacy of reading these texts in context, as only one part of the whole body of Scripture. This is the leap of faith which enables us to read ourselves into the audience and to hear the texts as if they were addressed to each of us without regard to gender.

NATIONALISM IN PROVERBS?

If the emphasis of the words which are often translated "loose woman" or "adventuress" falls more on "foreign-ness" than on gender, as I have suggested above, then the contributors to Proverbs might seem to advocate an ethnic exclusiveness which is also an inadequate basis for those who want to learn to live out their lives in accordance with God's intentions. It may be a misunderstanding to read "foreignness" or "otherness" in terms of nationality. When Jeremiah accused Israel of having abandoned the LORD in order to chase after other gods, he says that the LORD planted a faithful seed but got a "foreign" vine (Jer. 2:21; RSV "wild"). "Otherness" thus seems to refer in Jeremiah's time to idolatry or apostasy rather than to nationality. In later centuries we find the same tendency expressed in a wisdom poem from the fourth cave at Qumran, which describes certain aspects of the generalized concept of evil in terms of a harlot's wiles.

Thus, I suggest once again that it is essential to judge and evaluate the opinions represented by the wise over against the rest of the biblical canon. The speaker in Isa. 56:1-8 (for instance) proclaims an ethnically inclusive vision of God's intentions. Such diversity within the canon should indicate to the reader of the whole Scriptures that any hostility towards other ethnic groups which may be perceived in Proverbs should be understood as descriptive of a culturally and historically limited reality. This and related issues will be discussed further in the body of the Commentary, particularly in relationship to Prov. 2:16-19; 5:1-23; 7:10-27; 31:10-31.

A Commentary on the Book of
Proverbs

CONTENTS

WHO KNOWS WHAT IS GOOD?

INTRODUCTION:
THE SHAPE OF
THE LITERATURE

THE MEANING OF MASHAL

Most of us come to our reading of the biblical book of Proverbs assuming that we know what a "proverb" is. We might find it difficult to define the term, but most of us could come up with several examples of the short, catchy sayings which pass for proverbs in our own language. Thus, when we see that our English translations of the book begin with the heading "the proverbs of Solomon," we might expect for the heading to be followed by a collection of sayings similar to our own culture's "Penny wise, pound foolish," or "A stitch in time saves nine." However, the Hebrew word *mashal,* which is translated into the English word "proverb," has a wider range of meaning in Hebrew than it does in English. *Mashal* is indeed used in some parts of the OT to refer to short, popular (or traditional) sayings corresponding to the English meaning of "proverb." David is said to have quoted "a proverb" of this type to Saul (1 Sam. 24:13). But the word also refers in some contexts to a taunt or a negative-example saying (which RSV translates "byword," as in Deut. 28:37 or Jer. 24:9). Furthermore, *mashal* is used in several OT contexts to describe relatively lengthy speeches or discourses (as in Job 27:1; 29:1 or Num. 24:3, 15, 20, 21, 23).

Thus we should not be overly surprised to find that the book we call Proverbs contains other forms of literature in addition to short or "proverbial" sayings. In fact, only a little more than half of the material preserved for us in this book bears any resemblance to the conventional meaning given to the English word "proverbs."

17

"Solomonic Sayings"

Most of the sayings which resemble our traditional notions of a "proverb" are found grouped together in Prov. 10:1–22:16 and 25:1–29:27. Although the sayings are sometimes loosely connected according to theme or topic (e.g., 26:13-16 concerns "sluggards"), there is often no continuity of thought between adjacent verses. A collection of such disconnected bits of information as this may be referred to as "sentence literature," as the basic sense unit is seldom longer than a sentence. But, since both of the major "sayings" sections begin with a repetition of the heading "the proverbs of Solomon" (though 25:1 adds "which the men of Hezekiah king of Judah copied"), some scholars argue that the headings should be understood as a name given to a recognized type or subgroup within the larger heading of *mashal*.

For convenience, we will refer to the units in these sections as "Solomonic sayings," but the phrase ought to be understood as a formal designation (indicating a type of utterance) rather than an attribution of authorship. According to 1 Kgs. 4:32, Solomon was widely known for the large number of "proverbs" that he "uttered." However, the text does not indicate whether he was thought to have composed or invented what he "uttered," so the reference does not necessarily mean that he originated either the type or this specific collection of sayings. Whether such sayings originated anonymously from the general populace (as folk proverbs seem to do) or whether they were the deliberate composition of one or more individual representatives of wisdom in Israel, they have now been incorporated into the body of literature which the community of faith affirms as sacred Scripture. It is within that context that we will attempt to understand their meanings and their functions.

The Longer Poetic Units

The two major collections of "Solomonic sayings" cited above are surrounded (and separated from each other) by less cryptic, more personal, and more lengthy literary units which might be better described as poems or as poetic "speeches" rather than "proverbs" in the English sense of the word. These longer units use pairs of parallel lines similar to those found in the shorter sayings, but they use them as "building blocks" in the construction of more complex utterances in which continuity of thought between the pairs in a given unit can be easily recognized. Such poetic units make up the framework (the beginning, the middle, and the end) of the entire book of Proverbs. The longer poetic units fall into several different sub-categories according to content, structure, and tone.

INSTRUCTIONS

A number of the longer units begin with a direct form of address (in contrast to the third person format of the "Solomonic sayings") and are formulated as if they were the counsel of a teacher or a parent directed to a pupil or a child. Thus, for example, Prov. 2, 3, 5, 6, and 7 are all addressed to an individual whom the speaker calls "my son" (or "O sons" in 4:1; 5:7; 7:24).

Such advice-giving compositions are usually called Instructions. As a type of literature they are not unique to Israel, but follow a form which was known and used throughout the ancient world. A dozen or more Egyptian Instructions with a similar structure have been identified, and some of the Egyptian texts also have contents which parallel the subject matter of Proverbs.

The Instructions in Prov. 1–9 make frequent use of the second person imperative (the command form) of the verbs (e.g., give heed, trust, honor, avoid, put away, give, go). They are directly addressed to the wisdom student and advise, urge, and plead with the student to "listen" and follow the speakers' directions. However, within the larger context of these Instructions, the careful reader may recognize a variety of other types of literature which have been worked into the advice-giving framework. For instance, some lines within the longer compositions sound like popular sayings which have been incorporated into a larger structure (e.g., "in vain is a net spread in the sight of any bird" in 1:17; or "stolen water is sweet" in 9:17). Some units (e.g., 9:1-6) might be better described as poetic allegories, and some use first person speeches put into the mouths of personified wisdom or folly (e.g., 1:22-33).

Although the Hebrew text does not number the distinguishable units, this commentary will refer to twelve Instructions (divided on the basis of form and content) in the first nine chapters of Proverbs. The reader should be aware, however, that there is a great deal of scholarly disagreement over how the materials should be divided for discussion.

Each of the twelve Instructions considered in the following commentary begins with an appeal for the "son" or "sons" to pay attention to the advice that is being given. Each unit is limited to a single subject. A new Instruction begins when a change of subject occurs along with a repetition of the heading. However, within the units themselves, the terms "son" and "sons" are also used parenthetically, for emphasis without a change of subject (as in 1:8, 10, 15).

PERSONIFICATIONS

In 1:20-33 and in most of chs. 8 and 9 the form of the longer poetic units varies from that of the Instructions. In these units both wisdom and folly are personified: they are pictured as if they were women engaging in human forms of activity. Instead of a direct form of address from the teacher to the pupil, the personifications begin with a narrative description of entities who have a kind of autonomy apart from the teacher. Wisdom personified takes on a life of her own. She can gesture, move, reason, and speak for herself. She becomes the epitome of the wisdom teacher, and the twelfth and final Instruction is put into her mouth (8:32-36).

"SAYINGS OF THE WISE"

The material collected together in 22:17–24:34 has a didactic or "instructional" slant, but its formal characteristics differ somewhat from the Instructions in chs. 1–9. This section, called "the words of the wise" or the "sayings of the wise" (from the headings in 22:17 and 24:23), consists of two collections of sayings which are longer and more loosely formed than the Solomonic sayings but shorter and more diverse than most of the Instructions in chs. 1–9 or 31. The first "sayings of the wise" collection (22:17–24:22) consists of a prologue and thirty sayings (most of which take two verses to complete). A number of parallels can be found between this section of material and an Egyptian collection known as the Instruction of Amenemope.

THE WORDS OF AGUR AND OF LEMUEL'S MOTHER

Chapter 30 (which the text refers to as the "words of Agur") also differs in form and content from the rest of the literature in the book of Proverbs. The chapter contains a number of "graded numerical sayings" and refers to the deity as *Eloah* rather than LORD. We will consider the contents of this section and its various forms of expression in the Commentary itself.

Chapter 31 is said to contain the "words of Lemuel's mother." The first nine verses specifically counsel a king (or a future king) concerning the responsibilities of a ruler. Verses 10-31 may or may not be a part of the mother's speech. Since its form is unique, we will list it separately here, but it will be discussed in the Commentary as a part of the Words of Lemuel's Mother.

THE POETIC CONCLUSION (31:10-31)

The book closes with a poem in the form of an alphabetic acrostic. In twenty-two verses, corresponding to the twenty-two letters of the Hebrew alphabet, someone (either Lemuel's mother or one of the wise ones in Israel) describes and glorifies "the ideal woman."

For convenience of discussion, the commentary which follows will divide the text of Proverbs into four sections: (1) chs. 1–9, made up of Instructions interspersed with personification passages, (2) the Solomonic sayings found in 10:1–22:16 and 25:1–29:27, (3) the "sayings of the wise" in 22:17–24:34, and (4) chs. 30–31, containing the sayings attributed to Agur and to Lemuel's mother and the poetic praise of the "ideal woman."

SECTION ONE
PROVERBS 1:1–9:18

CHAPTER ONE

THE "TITLE" (1:1)

Like the title on the cover of a modern volume, the first verse of Proverbs serves as a shorthand designation for the literature which follows. While the title of a work sometimes describes its contents and occasionally refers to authorship, these are not primary functions. The true purpose of a title is to label the literature, to help readers distinguish one body of writings from another.

The phrase which is used for the title (*mishley shelomoh,* translated as "the proverbs of Solomon") is found again in 10:1 and 25:1, leading some critics to conclude that several different collections were known by the same title. However, it is also possible that by the time the entire book was put into its present form, the phrase "proverbs of Solomon" had become a generic designation for a particular type of saying. In either case it is likely that the heading was more concerned with labeling the material than it was with ascribing authorship to the individual units which follow.

THE "PROLOGUE" (1:2-7)

After the title comes a section which serves the same purpose as a prologue in a modern work: it is addressed to the audience in general, and it precedes the main body of material. This "prologue" sets the stage and provides the audience with the proper context for understanding everything which follows. Verses 2-4 should be understood as dependent clauses which hang on the advice given in v. 5. Similarly, v. 6 is dependent upon v. 7 for the completion of its thought. Taken together, as a "prologue" to the whole, these verses advise potential readers concerning the best way to make use of the diverse material the book contains.

Both the untutored and those who have already acquired a certain measure of wisdom are advised to pay attention to what follows. The wise can never sit back and assume that their wisdom is complete. As long as there are situations in life requiring decisions ("wise dealing, righteousness, justice, and equity," v. 3), the wise can "increase in learning." And as long as there are new pupils to be taught, the wise can continue to improve in the ways they hand on what they know to the young or to "the simple." Whether you are one of the wise or not, the prologue wants you to remember that an adequate understanding of the proverbs, the figures, the riddles, or the words of the wise, must begin with "the fear of the LORD" (v. 7a). When the term "fear of the LORD" is used in other OT texts, it refers both to the sense of awe human beings feel in the presence of the LORD and to the respect they show towards the LORD's intentions and teachings.

The prologue, then, specifies the attitude with which the reader should come to the reading of "the words of the wise" and concludes that only fools would dare to ignore this bit of advice (v. 7b). Everything which follows should be understood as being based on the prior assumption of respect, reverence, and fidelity towards the LORD.

WHEN SINNERS ENTICE YOU

The First Instruction (1:8-19)

The form of speech changes in v. 8 from a descriptive statement of purpose addressed to any or all readers (in vv. 2-7) to an imperative directed towards a specific individual. This is the first of a long series of commands or exhortations addressed to "my son." The casual reader might assume that Solomon is speaking here to one of his children. However, in the Hebrew Bible the terms "father" and "son" are often used metaphorically to refer to a teacher-student relationship (e.g., 2 Kgs. 2:3-5, 12). There are indications that the headmasters of schools in other ancient Near Eastern cultures were called "school-fathers" and that their pupils were called "school-sons" (Marvin R. Wilson, *Our Father Abraham*, 280). Thus, "my son" may have been simply a conventional form of address (the way wisdom teachers ordinarily spoke to their pupils). It is unclear from the context whether the third person reference to the parent's role (not "listen to *me*" but "listen to *your father's* instruction") is simply a roundabout way of speaking or whether it indicates that someone other than the parent is speaking. It is possible that we should understand the speaker here to be personified wisdom (as clearly is the case in Prov. 8:32), speaking through the voice of the wisdom teacher and calling her pupils by the customary title "son."

Hebrew poetry involves the rhyming of ideas or thoughts rather than sounds. This poetic technique is referred to as "parallelism." In 1:8 the parallel terms are synonymous (one idea is stated in two slightly different ways). "Hear" and "reject not" are roughly equal in meaning, as are "father's instruction" and "mother's teaching." The word translated here as "teaching" is the Hebrew word *torah,* which is often mistakenly understood as "law" rather than as education. The use of *torah* here in combination with the command to "hear" (from Heb. *shemaʿ,* meaning "listen!" or "pay attention!") may remind the audience of the passages in Deuteronomy which urge the people of Israel to hear and to teach the LORD's *torah* to their children and to their children's children. The speaker here may have intended to remind the audience of what Moses said: "Behold, I have taught you statutes and ordinances, as the LORD my God commanded me. . . . Keep them and do them; for that will be your wisdom and your understanding in the sight of the peoples . . ." (Deut. 4:5a, 6a). Since the prologue makes such a point of presupposing "the fear of the LORD," it would not be unreasonable to assume that the "mother's *torah*" and the "father's instruction" were understood to be similar in content to the *torah* of Moses.

After urging him to pay attention to his parents' teachings, the speaker offers the "son" a reason for following this advice (Prov. 1:9). It is unclear whether the reason is that they (the teachings) will make him more attractive or whether the "garland" and "pendants" have some other significance, such as a sign of office or a mark of honor. It does seem evident, however, that this reason is quite different from the reasons Moses gave the people for following the LORD's *torah.*

Violence and Bloodshed (1:10-19)

The speaker turns in v. 10 from general to more specific advice, and the speech which follows the parenthetical use of "my son" seems almost modern in its references. Perhaps it is particularly significant that the first of the Instructions should recognize some of the ways in which greed and social (peer?) pressure can lead youngsters to forget the teachings of their parents. It would not be difficult to find present-day correspondences for this ancient piece of advice. We sometimes think that wanton violence is a phenomenon peculiar to our own times. But this passage indicates that people in the author's time were also familiar with both the senseless shedding of innocent blood (v. 11) and violence for personal gain (v. 13).

After graphically picturing the way temptation will present itself (in vv. 11-14), the speaker urges "my son" (used parenthetically again in v. 15) to run the other way. The sum of the argument is expressed in the form of a "popular proverb" in v. 17, which seems to make the point that even birds are able to avoid a visible trap.

Wisdom (or the wisdom teacher) knows and tries to persuade us that violence itself is a trap which "takes away the life of its possessors." Thus, violence has the opposite effect from wisdom, which is said elsewhere to give life to its adherents.

Once again, the language and spirit of the speech reminds us of Deuteronomic sermons which warn the people of God against allowing themselves to be "enticed" away from the love and the fear of the LORD (e.g., Deut. 13:6ff.).

WISDOM PERSONIFIED (1:20-33)

Two verses (Prov. 1:20-21) introduce the next major section, making sure that we know that what follows comes directly from the mouth of Wisdom. Through the literary technique we call personification, wisdom seems to take on a life of its own. In vv. 20-33 Wisdom speaks of herself in the first person, as though she were a woman. The word which is translated Wisdom (with a capital W) has the form of a feminine plural noun in the Hebrew text. Since the Hebrew plural is often used to indicate an abstract concept, we might conclude from her name that this figure represents all wisdom wrapped into one symbolic character. Claudia V. Camp points out that the technique of personification calls attention to the unity of the subject. The metaphorical integrity of Wisdom encourages the audience "to seek the underlying unity of the multi-faceted expression of the proverb collection" (*Wisdom and the Feminine in the Book of Proverbs*, 215).

John J. Collins also suggests that when we hear Wisdom speaking as a person "we are being told that it is not simply a human achievement. We do not simply acquire wisdom by our own efforts" (*Proverbs, Ecclesiastes,* 17). To a certain extent, wisdom is thought of here as a gift (as 2:6 will state explicitly), rather than as a human attribute. However, subsequent speeches indicate that assertiveness and initiative are also required from the seeker after wisdom (cf. 4:5-6).

The woman known as Wisdom does not wait for people to come to her. She takes the initiative and cries out in the manner of an OT prophet, confronting people in the busiest parts of their lives (in the marketplaces, in the streets, at the city gates—where all the important concerns of the city would be discussed).

The phrase "how long" in 1:22 is more like an expletive or exclamation of impatience than a request for information (e.g., Num. 14:11; Job 18:2; 19:2; Ps. 13:1-2). Here Wisdom speaks to the "simple ones" who "love being simple" and to those who "hate knowledge" in the same terms that a prophet addresses those who turn away from the LORD and the LORD's ways. There are striking resemblances between Wisdom's speech in Prov. 1:22-33 and some of the classical prophets' sermons. Wisdom speaks through the wisdom teacher's voice in much the same way as the LORD speaks through the prophets of Israel and Judah.

If an audience were already familiar with the sermons of Amos, they would certainly be reminded here of the prophet's parallel phrasing: "They shall . . . seek the word of the LORD, but they shall not find it" (Amos 8:12). Wisdom's complaint in Prov. 1:24 sounds quite similar to Isa. 65:12, where the LORD says, "when I called, you did not answer, when I spoke, you did not listen . . ." (cf. Isa. 66:4).

The words in Prov. 1:22-27 are addressed directly to the rebels who spurn wisdom. But in v. 28 Wisdom seems to turn to another audience (perhaps to the person called "my son" in the previous section). She speaks in vv. 28-33 in the third person *about* rather than *to* those who ignore or reject her advice. The parallelism in v. 29 indicates clearly that the speaker equates "knowledge" with "the fear of the LORD." If one assumes that the knowledge referred to here is secular or ungodly, then this equation might seem blasphemous. But if the counsels of Wisdom and the *torah* of the LORD are understood as simply two ways of expressing the same truths, then the rejection of wisdom logically can be understood as a form of sin which is subject to the consequences of sin: "the simple are killed by their turning away, and the complacence of fools destroys them" (v. 32).

The word which is translated "simple" (in the RSV) implies an intentional avoidance of wisdom or knowledge rather than an inability to comprehend it. In Hosea God speaks to the priests of Israel through the prophet, saying, "My people are destroyed for lack of knowledge. . . . Since you have forgotten the law (literally, teachings, *torah*) of your God, I also will forget your children" (Hos. 4:6). Here in Proverbs the speaker first asserts that rejecting what Wisdom has to offer is virtually the same as refusing to give reverence to the LORD (Prov. 1:29) and then describes the consequences (vv. 28-33) of these foolish refusals to listen to Wisdom.

The final verse in this section also echoes a number of prophetic judgment speeches: the positive side, the rewards of "listening" to wisdom, are portrayed in glowing terms. The "me" in v. 33 has to be understood as Wisdom in this context, but it is clear that the same statement could be made with God as its subject. Nearly everything that is said about wisdom in this speech has been said about God in other parts of the Hebrew Scriptures. Again the reader must keep constantly in mind the assumption (which is explicitly articulated in 2:6) that wisdom is the gift of God to humankind. The rejection of the Gift (Wisdom) may be understood as a symbol for the rejection of the Giver.

CHAPTER TWO

WISDOM AND FAITH ARE RELATED

The Second Instruction (2:1-22)

A repetition of "my son" marks the opening of a second major instructional speech. Although several subunits may be distinguished, a relatively coherent argument is carried through the entire chapter. Here the wisdom teacher pursues the idea that was put in Wisdom's own mouth in the preceding chapter: there are undeniable connections between the search for "wisdom" and the "fear of the LORD."

The Knowledge of God (2:1-15)

Again we hear echoes of well-known prophetic texts. The concept of "knowing" God plays an important part in the ministries of both Hosea and Isaiah. Hosea informs the people of Israel that the LORD has a grievance against them because "there is no faithfulness or kindness, and no knowledge of God in the land" (Hos. 4:1). In Isaiah the LORD says "Israel does not know, my people does not understand" (Isa. 1:3), and "therefore my people go into exile for want of knowledge" (Isa. 5:13). Here in Prov. 2:5, the speaker uses poetic parallelism to equate "the knowledge of God" with "the fear of the LORD" and argues (in vv. 1-5) that both can be achieved through an active pursuit of wisdom.

Both vv. 5-8 and vv. 9-10 begin with "then," implying that both are the results to be expected by those who fulfill the conditions given in vv. 1-4. A dedicated search for insight and understanding must lead one to the LORD, because the LORD is the source of all knowledge and understanding (v. 6). The teacher seems to imply that there is a reciprocal relationship between "upright" behavior

31

and wisdom: either one leads its possessors to the other. Just as the pursuit of wisdom leads us to the knowledge of God, it also leads us to understand what righteousness, justice, and equity are all about (v. 9). It is the teacher's conviction that having wisdom in one's heart is closely tied to being one of the LORD's faithful followers.

Modern readers sometimes define wisdom so narrowly that they cannot see any relationship between it and the faithful worship of the LORD. But those who have collected and preserved these traditions for us insist that wisdom must be seen through the lenses of faith. We ought to take seriously this speaker's assertion that wisdom and worship are two sides of the same "coin." Wisdom enables and encourages us to act in life-enhancing ways that are fully in accord with the *torah* (i.e., the teachings) of our LORD.

Although the RSV makes it difficult to see, the Hebrew indicates that the thought begun in v. 10 is continued in v. 12 and again in v. 16. The logic of the argument seems to be that having wisdom in one's "heart" acts as a protective device, because wisdom includes the knowledge of God, or knowing what God is about. Thus those who have discretion and understanding will be "delivered" (v. 12) or "saved" (v. 16) from evil influences. Two types of evil are specified here: "men of perverted speech" who "delight in the perverseness of evil" and what the RSV calls "the loose woman" who "forgets the covenant of her God."

Temptation Personified (2:16-19)

Hebrew has a number of specific terms which describe various kinds of sexual infidelity, but neither of the words which the RSV translates in v. 16 as "loose woman" and " adventuress" falls into that category. The reference is to temptations inherent in non-Israelite (and non-Yahwistic) connections. Both words in this verse have the literal sense of "outsider" *(zarah)* or "foreigner" *(nokriya)*.

In Exod. 2:22 and 18:3 Moses refers to his son's being born in a "foreign" *(nokriyah)* land, and in 1 Kgs 11:1 we are told that Solomon brought many "foreign" women into his household. Jeremiah uses *nokriya* to refer to apostasy (turning away from the LORD, towards "strange" gods), but by far the most common usage of *nokriyah* as an adjective applied to women is found in

Ezra. When Ezra wanted to free the postexilic community from "contaminating" (non-Yahwistic) influences, he insisted that all marriages with "foreign women" be dissolved (cf. Ezra 10:2, 10, 11, 14, 17, 18, 44). Those who remained "outsiders" to the covenant community could not remain married to those who were loyal to their covenant with God.

In a similar way, the word *zarah* comes from a root meaning "strange" or "profane" and usually refers to religious (rather than sexual) infidelity, as in Deut. 32:16 or Ps. 44:20. In Prov. 2:16-19 the woman is said to have forgotten the covenant with her God, lending support to a religious rather than a sexual understanding of her wickedness.

Thus, when they are found in other OT passages the words *nokriyah* and *zarah* refer to "otherness" or "alienness," in a religious or a cultural and ethnic sense. There are no sexual or moral innuendos inherent in the words themselves. However, it is clear that in this passage, as well as in several other sections of Proverbs, the "foreign woman" plays a seductive role. Here in Proverbs, indirect references to sexual infidelity may be used as a metaphor (as in Hosea) for abandoning the covenant of the LORD. Or perhaps, by analogy, the terms meaning "outsider" are being used to refer to one who acted outside the bonds of marriage, rather than (or as well as) those who were "outside" the covenant with the LORD. But it is also possible that this particular wisdom teacher shares Ezra's conviction that foreign ways are as tempting to the "unwise" as sexual lures.

In any case it is clear that the "alien woman" personifies the exact opposite of "wisdom," and the teacher claims that her "paths" lead the unsuspecting down towards death rather than life. However, the speaker assures us that "discretion" can "save" us from falling into "alien" ways. This attitude towards the outsider would not have been unique to Israel. An Egyptian wisdom document known as the Instruction of Ani includes similar advice: "Be on thy guard against a woman from abroad, who is not known in her (own) town. . . . Do not know her carnally: a deep water, whose windings one knows not, a woman who is far away from her husband. 'I am sleek,' she says to thee every day. She has no witnesses when she waits to ensnare thee" (*ANET,* 420). (For further discussion of the "temptress," see below on 7:5-27.)

Summary (2:20-22)

The conclusion of the argument summarizes what has been said before: listening to wisdom leads to right behavior (i.e., being "upright"), and "the upright will inhabit the land." But lack of wisdom has all the opposite results.

CHAPTER THREE

The Torah of Wisdom
The Third Instruction (3:1-20)

References to both God (3:4) and LORD (vv. 5, 7, 9,) and use of traditional covenantal language make this passage sound more religiously oriented than previous units. The phrase "my son" in v. 11 is used for rhetorical effect and is not the start of a new Instruction. The subject of the blessings to be gained by an appropriate attitude towards wisdom runs throughout the unit.

Loyalty and Faithfulness (3:1-4)

The speaker in 3:1-4 does not specify that the "loyalty" and "faithfulness" he refers to are related to the covenant between God and Israel. But it is hard to imagine that anyone acquainted with OT covenant traditions could avoid seeing such connotations in the text. The words used here for "loyalty" (*hesed*) and "faithfulness" (*emet*) are frequently paired in OT texts. Only on very rare occasions do they seem to refer to noncovenantal human relationships (such as in Gen. 24:49 or 47:29). By far the most common usage is in contexts referring to the qualities of God as they are demonstrated through God's relationship with Israel. Thus, according to Exod. 34:6 Moses discovered on Mt. Sinai that the LORD was "abounding in steadfast love and faithfulness" (*hesed* and *emet*).

The Psalms repeatedly praise the LORD for having manifested this pair of attributes (e.g., Ps. 25:10; 86:15; 115:1; 117:2; 136). But God's chosen people were also expected to respond to the love they had been given by showing *hesed* and *emet* to each other. Hosea highlights their failure to do so in his accusation against

35

Israel: "There is no *emet* and no *hesed,* and no knowledge of God in the land" (Hos. 4:1). And Isaiah envisions the time when "a throne will be established in steadfast love *(hesed)* and on it will sit in faithfulness *(emet)* in the tent of David one who judges and seeks justice and is swift to do righteousness" (Isa. 16:5).

It seems clear, then, that similarities in subject and in forms of expression must have forced early audiences to see some connection between these admonitions in Proverbs and the covenant they believed God had made with their ancestors. However, there are also noticeable departures from (or modifications of) the tradition. For instance, in Deuteronomy the human partners to the covenant were urged to keep copies of the statutes and ordinances of the covenant in prominent places, "binding" them like ornaments around their heads and hands. But in Prov. 3:3, it is the abstract quality of "loyalty and faithfulness" rather than the very specific commandments which the "son" is urged to "bind" around his neck. Rather than on tablets of stone, a metaphorical "tablet" of one's "heart" (which might better be translated "mind," since the Hebrew word connotes the seat of human decision making) is the place in which the wisdom teacher's commandments should be kept (cf. Jer. 31:33).

"Be Not Wise In Your Own Eyes" (3:5-18)

The resemblances to Deuteronomy continue in Prov. 3:5ff. Deuteronomy says, "Know then in your heart that, as a man disciplines his son, the LORD your God disciplines you" (Deut. 8:5). Prov. 3:11-12 not only echoes the thought but also uses the same root for the word translated "discipline" *(ysr)*. Prov. 3:9 commands the listener to offer the "first fruits" of all his crops to the LORD, as does Deut. 26:2ff., and promises material rewards for obedience, as do many other portions of Deuteronomy. Again, however, a distinct departure from Yahwistic tradition occurs in Prov. 3:13-20, where wisdom is raised to something approaching divine status: "Long life is in her right hand" (v. 16), and "She is a tree of life to those who lay hold of her" (v. 18). Some critics have suggested that this combination of similarities and dissimilarities indicates an attempt on the part of the wisdom teacher(s) to set wisdom precepts up as a rival to the *torah* given to Israel by God.

It is evident, however, that as the text now stands vv. 5-7 ("Trust

in the LORD. . . . Be not wise in your own eyes; fear the LORD,
and turn away from evil") set the tone for the reading of the more
problematic passages. We should come to the reading of vv. 13-20
already primed with the assumption that human insight comes
from and is accountable to the LORD.

Wisdom Is the LORD's Tool (3:19-20)

If the preceding verses had tempted us to set wisdom on too high
a pedestal, vv. 19-20 would serve as a timely reminder that wisdom
is subordinate to the LORD, as any instrument or agent is subordinate to the one who wields it. The LORD and not wisdom is the
ultimate source of life. Taken as a whole, the Instruction blends a
concern for prudence (an awareness of a relationship between acts
and their results) with an affirmation that human wisdom alone is
not a sufficient basis for all actions.

SIGNPOSTS ALONG THE WAY

The Fourth Instruction (3:21-35)

In the previous chapter the way of wisdom was pictured as the
polar opposite of the way of wickedness. The contrasts between
the two paths and their destinations were starkly drawn. Perhaps
the teacher was oversimplifying in order to get a point across. Most
of us know that in real life such clear-cut distinctions are more
difficult to make. Very few courses of action (in the modern world,
at least) fit so neatly into absolutely right or wrong categories.
Experience teaches us that we cannot easily tell where a particular
path will lead us. It is this apparent overconfidence in predicting
the consequences of actions which Qohelet will object to most
strongly in the second half of Ecclesiastes. Here in the fourth
Instruction, the wisdom teacher assures us that some directional
signals are available. In fact the teacher implies that this is what
commandments and precepts are for: they function as signposts
along the way, enabling the wise to discern the direction in which
they are headed. Thus, those who keep an eye on "wisdom and
discretion" can walk confidently along uncertain paths secure in the
LORD's protection (vv. 21-26) and guided by some specific direc-
tives (vv. 27-31).

Four verses, each consisting of two antithetical lines, make up the conclusion of this set of instructional speeches. Although most of the material in chs. 1–9 is expressed in longer thought units, the technique seen here involving the "rhyming" of ideas in short parallel phrases will become the dominant style in chs. 10–22.

CHAPTER FOUR

A FATHER'S ADVICE

The Fifth Instruction (4:1-9)

The fifth Instruction is addressed to "sons" (or children), in the plural. The gender of the advice-giving speaker is made clear here for the first time through the phrase "when I was a son with my father" (4:3). Here, also, the "father" takes some care to specify that he was not the originator of the *torah* he propounds. It was handed down to him by his own father, along with the understanding that the relationship between Wisdom and her lovers is reciprocal: "Do not forsake her, and she will keep you; love her, and she will guard you" (v. 6).

WICKEDNESS IS ADDICTIVE

The Sixth Instruction (4:10-19)

The sixth speech emphasizes the need to keep to the straight and narrow, never to swerve from the paths of wisdom and uprightness (which are equated in v. 11). The paths of "the wicked" must be completely avoided (vv. 14-15), because evil ways, once begun, are addictive: the "wicked" cannot sleep "unless they have done wrong" (v. 16). Once tasted, wickedness and violence take the place of a staple diet (v. 17). Those who remember what they have been taught can proceed through life without fear of stumbling (vv. 12-13), because the path of the "righteous" gets brighter and brighter as they travel along it (v. 18). The wicked, however, trip in the dark over unknown obstacles (v. 19).

39

HOLISTIC HEALTH

The Seventh Instruction (4:20-27)

The seventh Instruction restates the point of the sixth, using the names of a number of body parts to describe the task confronting the wisdom pupil. In vv. 20-22 the health (RSV "healing") of the whole body (RSV "flesh") is said to depend on the diligent application of ears, eyes, and heart to the task of learning what the teacher has to teach. The Hebrew word *leb/lebab* (translated "heart") can also be translated "mind" because its range of meaning in Hebrew includes concepts we often associate with the word "mind" in English. The "heart/mind" represents the place within the human body where both rational and emotional decisions are made. In vv. 23-27 the instructor's advice encompasses the heart (v. 23), the mouth and lips (v. 24), the eyes (v. 25), and the feet (vv. 26-27). Each part named represents an activity which ought to be governed by wisdom teachings. Only a concerted effort by the whole person can succeed at wisdom's task. Both speeches in ch. 4 are concerned with the need to acquire and to hold on to wisdom instruction in order to avoid the pitfalls inherent in life, and both advise the learner to take an active part (using body, heart, and mind) in keeping to the right path.

CHAPTER FIVE

Don't Scatter Your "Springs" Abroad

The Eighth Instruction (5:1-23)

The eighth Instruction warns the wisdom student once more of dangers facing those who have "intercourse" with "strangers." Here, as in ch. 2, the translators of the RSV give moral-value connotations to the feminine forms of words which really mean "foreign." Thus, *zarah* is translated as "loose woman" in 5:3 and 20, while its masculine counterpart is simply rendered "strangers" in v. 10. And *nokriyah* is rendered "adventuress" in v. 20, while its masculine counterpart is merely said to be "alien" in v. 10. This bias may reflect the worldview of modern translators as much as it reflects the worldview of the original speaker.

On one level of reading (particularly with the help of the translators' biases), ch. 5 can be understood as a sermon advocating fidelity in marriage. Many modern audiences find it easier to identify with the message of the text at that level. Most of us prefer not to dwell on those periods in Israel's history when circumstances (and/or peoples' inclinations) led our ancestors to see all relationships with "outsiders" as sinful and destructive. However, a more or less neutral translation of the words *zarah* and *nokriyah* will indicate that here, as in other passages which refer to the foreign or the alien woman, sexual imagery is used metaphorically, as a figure for the lure of foreign ways. The fidelity which most concerns the speaker in Proverbs is fidelity to Israelite ways in a context where foreign ways are both overwhelmingly present and fatally attractive.

As Bitter as Wormwood (5:1-6)

The parenthetical "And now, O sons" in v. 7 divides the Instruction into two parts, each containing a similar warning. The first warning (vv. 1-6) closely parallels 2:16-19. If "lips" in 5:3 is taken as a figure for speech, then both passages recognize that the "words" of the foreigner are attractive. They seem to promise something desirable, but in fact they lead those who follow them "to Sheol" (5:5; cf. 2:18). (For a discussion of possible meanings for "Sheol" in the OT, see the Appendix to Ecclesiastes, pp. 203ff. below). We know that some postexilic leaders (such as Nehemiah or Ezra) thought that foreign women posed a threat to the Jewish community. And it is clear that the Deuteronomic authors who reflected on the history of Israel thought that the road which led their people to exile had been paved with idolatrous practices—practices which had been learned from the "aliens" with whom the Israelites had mingled in the land of Canaan. Nehemiah says that even Solomon, with all his power and wisdom, sinned because "foreign women" tempted him to do so (Neh. 13:26).

Drink Water From Your Own Cistern (5:7-23)

The second warning may be based on the traditional understanding that one had to be born of a Jewish mother in order to be considered a Jew. If Jewish men married non-Jewish women, their children would be lost to the community of faith. They too would become outsiders. Thus, the wisdom teacher points out that any energy invested in a mixed marriage will profit "strangers" (Prov. 5:10a) rather than Israelites or the community covenanted to the LORD and that the children born of such a liaison will belong to "the house of an alien" (v. 10b) rather than to the house of Israel or to the house of the LORD. Those who disregard the warnings of their teachers will "groan" at the end of their lives (v. 11), realizing (when it is too late) where their lack of "discipline" has led them (v. 12).

In case the "sons" addressed in v. 7 have not yet been fully convinced of the folly of foreign entanglements, the wisdom teacher adds a clincher to his argument: our ways are being observed by the LORD (v. 21). And since this is so, those who show "lack of discipline" (equated in v. 23 with "folly") are "lost." They will be "caught in the toils" of their own sins (v. 22).

The various references to water in vv. 15-18 are transparently sexual allusions, as vv. 18-20 make clear. But vv. 15-20 contain more than a simple warning against adultery. The repeated use of the Hebrew words meaning "foreign" in vv. 10, 17, and 20 make it probable that the advice given in *this* section is more concerned with national and religious identity than it is with personal morality. Very similar language is used in Jeremiah to describe the people's disloyalty to Yahweh: "They have forsaken me, the fountain of living waters," says the LORD, "and hewed out cisterns for themselves, broken cisterns, that can hold no water" (Jer. 2:13). Later in the same speech, Jeremiah asks the people what they think they have gained "by going to Egypt, to drink the waters of the Nile," or "by going to Assyria, to drink the waters of the Euphrates" (Jer. 2:18). In this section of Proverbs, as in the book of Jeremiah, the primary concern is with loyalty to the covenant between God and Israel. Specific references to adultery will be made, however, in the next chapter (see Commentary below on Prov. 6:20–7:27).

CHAPTER SIX

PARTICULAR PITFALLS

The Ninth Instruction (6:1-19)

The use of "my son" in 6:1 and 20 divides the chapter into two larger speeches (the ninth and tenth Instructions). The ninth Instruction deviates from the usual format when it begins with direct advice rather than with an admonition to pay attention to what is being said. There are four distinct subunits within 6:1-19. Each contains a warning against specific types of behavior. There is only one reference to the LORD in this speech (in v. 16), and the consequences that are said to follow from specific actions sound like natural rather than supernaturally imposed consequences.

Rash Pledges (6:1-5)

If, says the speaker to the listener, you have in some unthinkingly altruistic moment promised to be responsible for someone else's debts, you must do whatever you can to get out of the trap you have set for yourself. Beg, weep, and grovel if necessary. The wisdom teacher's attitude towards the dangers involved in "co-signing" a loan is ruthlessly pragmatic. This intransigent attitude stands in stark contrast to the views expressed in the Wisdom of Jesus ben Sirach, an apocryphal (or deuterocanonical) book which was never accepted into the Hebrew canon. Sirach (a Jewish sage of the 2nd cent. B.C.E.) acknowledges the problems lenders sometimes have in recovering their loans, but advises the faithful to go ahead and "lose your silver for the sake of a brother or a friend" (Sir. 29:10).

44

Excessive Slumber (6:6-11)

Those of us who would like to sleep a little later in the morning are warned that poverty sneaks up on sluggards like a thief in the night! A duplication of Prov. 6:10-11 occurs in the "Words of the Wise" section (24:33-34). In 6:6-8, as in the "Words of Agur" (30:25), the ant is held up as a worthy model of foresight and industry. Perhaps this section should be understood to refer back to the warnings against "surety." In 6:3-4 those who "are in their neighbors' power" are advised "to give their eyes no sleep" until they have disengaged themselves from their commitments. If one is ensnared "like a bird" in "the hand of a fowler," then the strictures against indulging in "a little sleep, a little slumber, a little folding of the hands to rest" (v. 10) seem appropriate in their context.

Crooked Speech (6:12-15)

Since gestures vary in meaning from culture to culture, we can only guess at what significance the body language described here might have had in its original social context. It is evident however, that whatever *is* done is done with evil intent, in order to deceive or to stir up trouble.

Things that the LORD Hates (6:16-19)

The speaker here uses a poetic device known as "sequential numbering" to name some specific forms of behavior which are condemned as "abominations" to the LORD. The form occurs again in 30:15-31, and can be seen in the oracles of Amos 1:3-2:8. Numerical sayings such as these usually begin by stating one number less than the total number of items to be named. Thus there are not six, but rather seven "things" named in Prov. 6:16-19. Nothing is said here about whether one should expect certain consequences to follow the doing of these "things which the LORD hates."

Both the allegorical reference to ants (in vv. 6-8) and the use of the sequential numbering style link ch. 6 with the "Words of Agur" in ch. 30.

WALK THE STRAIGHT AND NARRROW

The Tenth Instruction (6:20-35)

This speech begins with an exhortation which parallels the opening Instruction in 1:8-9. Here in ch. 6, the echoes of Deuteronomy are even stronger than they were in ch. 1. A comparison of Prov. 6:20-22 with Deut. 6:6-8 or 11:19 indicates resemblances which are so strong that coincidence cannot possibly explain them. Again, as in Prov. 1, the "son" is urged to remember both his father's commandments and his mother's teachings in order to avoid straying into dangerous territory. In ch. 1 violence was the danger to avoid. Here in ch. 6, it is illicit sex which poses a threat to the untutored.

Adultery Is Senseless (6:24-35)

In 6:24a the translation "evil woman" is possible from the Hebrew (MT), but a very small change in vowel pointing would make the phrase read "neighbor's wife" (as in v. 29). The words are nearly identical here with the commandment "you shall not covet your neighbor's wife" (Exod. 20:17). In fact, the Greek translators of the LXX understood the text in that way (as the NEB reflects in its rendering: "to keep you from the wife of another man"). Since the technical term for committing adultery *(no'eph)* actually does occur in Prov. 6:32, the Greek text (and the NEB) probably reflect the original sense more accurately. In v. 24b the RSV again renders the word *nokriyah* ("foreigner") as "adventuress" (as in 5:20).

Once more, in 6:26 the RSV (as also KJV, NIV, JB) translates a rather neutral term in Hebrew *(eshet ish,* meaning simply "a man's wife") with a negative-value word ("adulteress"). But there is really no reason to attribute sin to the woman mentioned here. The wisdom teacher is urging the "son" to avoid becoming sexually involved with a married woman, saying to him in effect, "You can hire a prostitute for a loaf of bread, but a married woman may cost you your life." The rest of the chapter is devoted to illustrating this very point. The teacher points out that jealousy inspires people with a burning desire for revenge (vv. 34-35), and one cannot play with fire without getting burnt (vv. 27-29). Furthermore argues the sage, adultery leaves one open to scorn. Those who steal food when they are starving are only punished—they are not despised by others. But those who "steal" sexual gratification will be dishonored as well as "wounded" (vv. 30-33).

God is not mentioned in this Instruction, and the reasons given for avoiding extramarital liaisons are purely practical. Anyone with "common sense" would want to avoid the consequences of being caught in adultery, but these consequences are described in natural terms (i.e., the spouse's anger). There is no hint at all here that God might monitor or punish such behavior. Nothing in this section indicates that the teacher was interested in the ethical or religious dimensions of adultery. The topic of adultery continues in the next chapter.

CHAPTER SEVEN

A HOUSE ON THE WAY TO SHEOL

The Eleventh Instruction (7:1-27)

The constant repetition of themes and variations on themes should be enough to persuade most readers that the instructional speeches represent an anthology or a collection of teachings addressed to an assortment of listeners (unless one thinks of the wisdom student as a remarkably slow learner). The eleventh Instruction contains yet another diatribe against illicit sex. While 6:26-35 had emphasized the natural consequences of adultery (the danger of a jealous spouse), this chapter speaks to those who feel that they are relatively safe from discovery. The teacher makes it clear that a jealous husband is not the only danger which threatens an adulterer. ✦

Call Wisdom Your Sister (7:1-5)

The Instruction begins with a familiar formula and repeats several phrases found in earlier speeches (e.g., "write them on the tablet of your heart" in 7:3b as in 3:3b, and "keep my commandments and live" in 7:2a as in 4:4b). Once again the advantages of cherishing wisdom (like a sister or an intimate friend) are stressed. In 7:5, as in 2:16 and 6:24, wisdom and insight are said to "preserve you from the *zarah* and the *nokriyah*" (which RSV is consistent in translating as the "loose woman" and the "adventuress" in all three passages).

A Twilight Encounter (7:6-23)

The narrative that begins in v. 6 paints a vivid picture. Through the speaker's eyes, we witness a seduction scene in which a "young

48

man without sense" (v. 7) is accosted by a "woman. . . dressed as a harlot" (v. 10). She is said to be both a foreigner (in v. 5) and to be married to another man (v. 19). The woman aggressively propositions the youth, who follows her home as unthinkingly "as an ox goes to the slaughter" (v. 22). Here, as in earlier passages dealing with the seductive powers of that which is forbidden, temptation is said to speak with "smooth words" (v. 5) and "smooth talk" (v. 21). But the "smoothness" of her argument does not rest in deception. The youth is not deceived about her marital status. After telling him what delights she has in store for him, the woman assures the gullible young man that they will not be risking discovery: her husband has gone away on a long trip. Thus, the persuasive power of her argument is not concerned with the rightness or the wrongness of their actions, but with their ability to evade detection. The young man's lack of wisdom leads him to believe that he can indulge in an illicit liaison without suffering any consequences. Only the "simple" and those who have ignored the teachings of wisdom are tempted to think that they can escape the repercussions of their actions.

The term "harlot" *(zonah)* is most frequently used in the OT as a figure for religious infidelity (e.g., Ezek. 16, 23). In both legal and prophetic texts "harlotry" usually refers either to participation in the Canaanite fertility cults or to any relationship the covenant people might have with "gods" other than Israel's LORD. Thus, the picture of the simpleton who is tempted by a woman dressed as a harlot may also allude to cultic apostasy.

Folly Is a Harsh Mistress (7:24-27)

The narrative in Prov. 7:6-23 speaks of the seduction incident as if it were simply a single encounter between individuals. But the conclusion in vv. 24-27 draws a more universalized moral than a single encounter would seem to merit. I suggest that the wisdom teacher knows that it is not just the act of adultery which leads to "death." Rather, believing that one can make choices which have no consequences leads to "death." This is the epitome of folly! It is Folly who has "laid low" many a victim (v. 26), and it is Folly's house which is "the way to Sheol" (in v. 27, as also in 9:13-18). Death can be understood here, as in some other parts of the OT, as a metaphor for separation or alienation from God. The wisdom

49

teacher would undoubtedly agree that the death to which Folly leads us is more fearsome than the mere cessation of bodily functions.

In contrast we are told that taking the words of the wisdom teacher seriously (i.e., remembering that all human beings are held accountable for their actions) leads to "life" (7:2). This contrast between life-giving wisdom and death-dealing folly makes a fitting prelude to Wisdom's self-introduction in the following chapter.

CHAPTER EIGHT

WISDOM SPEAKS FOR HERSELF

Does Not Wisdom Call? (8:1-3)

The first three verses of the chapter act as an introduction to Wisdom's own speech in the verses which follow. There are many parallels between 8:1-3 and 1:20-22. Both passages introduce us to Wisdom, personified as a woman. Both characterize her as one who actively seeks out followers. She is open and gregarious and not at all shy about advertising what she has to offer. She "cries aloud" from the hilltops, from the crossroads, from the city gates and entryways. The passage in ch. 1 begins with a declaration of fact, while this passage begins with a rhetorical question. The question expects the answer "Yes, of course." Everyone knows that wisdom is available! Both passages communicate the same message: those who remain unwise do so through choice—through their own refusal to listen to wisdom. However, the form of the word translated "wisdom" is not identical in both passages. In 1:20 the Hebrew word has the form of a feminine plural noun *(hokmot)* followed by feminine singular verb forms. Some scholars say this form is an "abstract plural" on the pattern of such words as *holelot* ("madness"), while others think it is a singular form on the pattern of the word for "sister" *(ahot)*. In any case it is clear that the word *hokmah,* used for Wisdom in 8:1, differs slightly from that used in 1:20. In 8:1 both the verbs and the noun *(hokmah)* are feminine singular in form.

Wisdom's speech in the remainder of ch. 8 falls roughly into two sections and a conclusion. The first section (vv. 4-21) is concerned with what Wisdom has to offer to her disciples. The second (vv. 22-31) refers to her credentials (what authorizes her to speak as she does). The conclusion in vv. 32-36 reminds us that when all is said and done, the voice of wisdom is the voice of the LORD.

51

My Cry Is to All Humankind (8:4-21)

In vv. 4-5 Wisdom stresses the universality of her invitation to discipleship. Her call is addressed to human beings in general (*beney adam,* v. 4b) and to the "simple" and the "foolish" in particular (v. 5). Wisdom assures us (vv. 6-9) that she speaks in a noble, righteous, and straightforward manner (unlike the seductive personage described in 7:10-23) and that she is unalterably opposed to "pride and arrogance . . . and perverted speech" (8:13).

Wisdom claims that what she has to offer is more valuable than silver, gold, or jewels (vv. 10-11, 18-19). The reference to "righteousness" and "justice" in v. 20 reframes the promise of wealth and full treasuries in v. 21. In its context the promise refers to something other than material rewards. What Wisdom has to offer is both different from *and* better than gold or silver.

It may be that the lure Wisdom holds out to those who love her is power. If so, it is power of a more durable nature than that which money can buy. Wisdom claims that it is her qualities, rather than wealth, which constitute the real strength behind any throne. All those who govern earthly realms depend on Wisdom to sustain their rules.

There seems to be one line too many in v. 13, and a statement about the fear of the LORD seems out of place in its present location where it interrupts what Wisdom is saying about herself in vv. 12-14. Thus, most scholars think the first line in v. 13 is a gloss (a reader's note which was later incorporated into the body of the text).

Wisdom Lists Her Credentials (8:22-31)

The second part of Wisdom's monologue answers an unspoken question: "Why should we believe wisdom's claims?" What makes Wisdom's promises more reliable than those made by the seductive personage described in the previous Instruction? Like the classical prophets who tell their skeptical listeners how they were called to the prophetic task, Wisdom tells her audience about her origins. In effect she says, "I trace my beginnings and my authority back to the LORD."

How Are Wisdom and the LORD Related?

The poetic device of personification creates some problems for the interpreter of this material. The poet has Wisdom speak as if she were a self-conscious entity. As a rhetorical device such personification has the effect of engaging the reader's emotions to a much higher degree than the mere discussion of an abstract concept could ever do. But the figure of speech leaves us unclear as to what it is that Wisdom represents in this passage. Should Wisdom be understood here as a *characteristic* of the LORD's creative activity or as a *companion* with a distinct identity? Is Wisdom represented as an originally independent divine being, or is she merely a figure of speech, standing for the collective traditions of the wise? Does Wisdom claim to have been created, begotten, or acquired by the LORD? Is her counsel helpful to humankind because she was *instrumental* in the creative process, or is she merely claiming to have been *present* at the world's inception? Arguments for one position or the other revolve around the correct way to understand several obscure and ambiguous phrases in vv. 22 and 30.

Ambiguities in 8:22

The word *qanani,* which the RSV translates "created me" in v. 22, could equally well mean "possessed me" (as an attribute or faculty) or "acquired me" (as one acquires a commodity). A number of biblical parallels can be found to support either translation. The biblical evidence for translating *qanani* as "begot me" is dubious (it would make sense only in Gen. 4:1). But there is a similar word in Ugaritic which means "procreate," and the use of birth-related language in Prov. 8:24-25 makes "begot me" a logically tempting alternative.

The phrase *re'shit darko,* which the RSV translates as "the beginning of his work," is a second stumbling block for the interpreter of v. 22. In Hebrew *re'shit* can mean either "first" (in time) or "first" (in importance). And while *darko* might be construed as "his work," it more commonly means "his way" or "his manner" of acting. The NAB, which renders *qanani* as "begot," translates *re'shit* with "firstborn."

The translations "created," "begotten," and "acquired" give readers the impression that Wisdom is presented here as an independent entity, apart from God. "Created" is favored by many, though the warrants for understanding the term in this way are relatively few. "Created" can imply that wisdom was simply the first of the LORD's creatures (e.g., R. N. Whybray, *Wisdom in Proverbs*, 100-101), whereas "acquired" implies that wisdom "pre-existed" and originated outside the created order (as Bruce Vawter argues in "Prov 8:22: Wisdom and Creation," 205-216).

However, understanding *qanani* in the sense of "possessed me" leaves open the possibility that Wisdom should be understood here as a personification of an attribute of God. Wisdom existed within God, prior to creation. Wisdom was a quality which the LORD demonstrated in the creation of the universe rather than an entity in its own right. As R. B. Y. Scott argues (*Proverbs–Ecclesiastes*, 71) "possess" is "clearly the meaning intended in the twelve other passages in Proverbs where the word is used" (e.g., Prov. 4:5-7). Reading *qanani* as "possessed me" would also bring the picture of Wisdom in 8:22ff. into line with the statement in 3:19: "The LORD by wisdom founded the earth; by understanding he established the heavens."

Begotten or Made?

Prov. 8:22-31 played an important part in early Christian debates about the nature of Christ. In the 4th cent. C.E. this passage was used both to support and to refute the Arians' claims. Assuming first that Christ could be equated with "the wisdom of God" (1 Cor. 1:24), the Arians argued that the Son, like Wisdom, was created. And to be a creature, whether the first or the most prominent of creatures, is to be subordinate to the Creator. But those who formulated the Nicean declaration that the Son was "begotten, not made" were inclined to translate *qanani* in Prov. 8:22 as "begot me" in order to argue that God and Christ were "consubstantial" (of the same essence and status).

Ambiguities in 8:30

Whether or not Wisdom seems to act as a co-equal, as a subordinate agent, or merely as an observer in the process of creation also depends on how one understands an obscure Hebrew word which the RSV translates "master workman" in v. 30. The meaning of *amon*, as it is presently vocalized in the MT, has been a subject of debate since ancient times. The word does not occur elsewhere in the Hebrew Scriptures in this form. Traditionally, interpreters have gone in one of two different directions for their translations, either (1) towards the image of "architect" or "artist" or (2) towards the idea of "infant" or "darling child." Either understanding involves a change in the vowels presently found in the MT, to *omman*, "artisan" (as in Cant. 7:2), or to *amun*, "nursling" (by analogy from the plural in Lam. 4:5).

The "artisan" advocates draw support from the deuterocanonical book known as the Wisdom of Solomon, which calls wisdom a "fashioner" or "craftsman" (Wis. 7:22; 8:6; 14:2 RSV). However, the proponents of the meaning "child" can point to the birth metaphors in Prov. 8:24-25 and to the reference to "delight" in the second part of v. 30 for corroboration. Those who prefer the reading "begot me" in v. 22 will of course argue for "child" in v. 30.

R. B. Y. Scott suggests that the original speaker intended the phrase to be read as *omen*, which would be an active participle, meaning one who unites or binds together. Thus, Scott translates v. 30a, "Then I was beside him binding [all] together" (*Proverbs–Ecclesiastes*, 68, 72). Scott's suggestion makes the word in question describe Wisdom's function in creation rather than her nature. However, if the participle refers to Wisdom's actions, one would expect it to have feminine form, which cannot be supported by the text. Other suggestions for understanding the term include "confidant" and "counselor," based on similar sounding words in languages closely related to Hebrew (see William McKane, *Proverbs*, 357-58). Of course, the underlying question with which the interpreters are concerned is whether Wisdom is here presented as an active agent participating in creation or whether she is pictured as merely an observer of the LORD's work. Roland E. Murphy sums up the interpreter's dilemma in a nutshell: "Lady Wisdom has received great press by reason of her association with creation, but her precise role remains unclear" ("Wisdom and Creation," 5).

Whether or not Wisdom claims to have been instrumental in the creative process, she clearly does say that she was *present* as the work was done. Thus, in spite of the ambiguities, her speech still functions to legitimate her teachings. In effect she says to those who question her credentials, "You can trust what I say about the

55

structures and the intricacies of life, because I was there to see how it was all put together in the first place."

CHOOSE LIFE!

The Twelfth Instruction (8:32-36)

The twelfth and final Instruction comes from the mouth of Wisdom herself, and once more wisdom, life, and the LORD are linked inextricably together. To find wisdom is to find life and "favor from the LORD" (v. 35). It is a clear matter of choice, and the choice is clear: "all who hate me love death" (v. 36). Just as Joshua told the people of Israel to "choose this day whom you will serve" (Josh. 24:15), Wisdom insists that we must choose either one path or the other. And, our teacher assures us, only the path of wisdom leads to "life."

CHAPTER NINE

ALTERNATE INVITATIONS

The contents of Prov. 9 could be considered a continuation of the twelfth Instruction, but the change from first person statements in 8:32-36 to third person statements about Wisdom in 9:1-3 makes such a linkage awkward. In ch. 9 the choice between life and death is presented to us one more time. Two allegories, separated by a short series of "Solomonic" maxims, lay out in graphic terms what Wisdom and Folly have to offer. Wisdom is described once again in vv. 1-3 and speaks for herself again in vv. 4-6 and 11-12. Folly is introduced in vv. 13-15 and speaks as a person in vv. 16-17. The RSV translation "a foolish woman" in v. 13 is misleading. The figure who speaks in vv. 16-17 is not just a randomly chosen fool. Rather, she represents the essence of the opposite of wisdom. The NIV and NAB recognize the personification intended with their rendering, "the woman Folly." The NEB translation "Lady Stupidity" is also worthy of note.

Like the seductive figure in ch. 7, both Wisdom and Folly offer to feed tempting morsels of food to their followers. In earlier chapters eating and drinking were used as euphemisms for sexual activity. There may still be suggestive overtones in the banquets offered here, but it is even more probable that food is offered in these two scenes as a gesture of hospitality. According to the customs of hospitality, those who "break bread together" share a common bond. The offer of hospitality is also an offer of protection to the otherwise unprotected. Both Wisdom and Folly invite the "simple" (i.e., those unprotected by knowledge of the world?) to "turn in here" (note the identical language in 9:4 and 16). But while the protection wisdom offers will lead to "life," the narrator

57

tells us in no uncertain terms that those who accept Folly's hospitality will end up "in the depths of Sheol" (v. 18).

The Intrusive Maxims (9:7-10)

Wisdom speaks of herself in the first person and addresses her listeners as "you" in vv. 5-6 and again in vv. 11-12. But vv. 7-10 interrupt Wisdom's monologue. They follow the third person style of generalization which characterizes the two-line parallelisms known as Solomonic proverbs. Only v. 10 seems to have any relevance to the subject matter of Wisdom's speech. The word "insight" *(binah)* occurs in both vv. 6 and 10. The "simple" are invited to follow "the way of insight" in v. 6, and the substance of which insight consists ("the knowledge of the Holy One") is spelled out in v. 10. However, the reference to the LORD in v. 10 makes it difficult to determine the antecedent of "me" in v. 11. The difficulties in reading this chapter can best be solved by assuming that v. 10 originated as a gloss (an early reader's comment upon the text) and that the maxims in vv. 7-9 have been carried over into this section from the Solomonic proverbs collection which begins in the following chapter.

The End of the Instructions (9:13-18)

The introductory framework section to the book of Proverbs (made up of the longer poetic units in chs. 1–9) comes to an abrupt end with the portrait of Folly drawn in 9:13-18. The reference to death and Sheol in v. 18 links Folly with the other temptations personified in 2:16-19; 5:3-6; and 7:10-27.

In this concluding episode, the teacher has Folly speak in the same open and public manner as Wisdom did in her previous appearances. In 9:16 Folly uses the same inviting words that Wisdom used in v. 4. And in v. 17 Folly tempts those who are "without sense" with what appears to be a bit of proverbial wisdom: "Stolen water is sweet, and bread eaten in secret is pleasant." One of the Solomonic sayings in the following section of the literature sounds quite similar: "Bread gained by deceit is sweet" (20:17). Again, "bread" and "water" may allude to illicit sex in these sayings as they did in chs. 5 and 6. These resemblances communicate a lesson: folly can be disguised as wisdom. Folly can be dressed in Wisdom's trappings and use Wisdom's ways to lure the unwary. In the first Solomonic sayings section (which begins in the following chapter) is a more concise statement of the same lesson: "there is a way which seems right to a man, but its end is the way to death" (16:25).

A Word to the Wise

By putting a proverb in Folly's mouth, the speaker both discredits its content and invites the listener to think more carefully and more critically about other sayings which popularly pass for truth. Thus, 9:13-18 makes a fitting introduction to the second major section of the book, which will consist almost entirely of short pithy sayings from which truth needs to be carefully sifted.

SECTION TWO
THE SOLOMONIC SAYINGS

Proverbs 10:1–22:16 and 25:1–29:27

THE FIRST COLLECTION (10:1–22:16)

With the end of ch. 9 and the beginning of ch. 10 the style of the literature changes radically. The personalized, cajoling, and didactic rhetoric of the Instructions gives way abruptly to the detached and impersonal generalizations of the sentence proverbs. The repetition of the phrase "the proverbs of Solomon" in 10:1 marks the beginning of a lengthy section in which sense units seldom consist of more than one verse. Each verse is capable of standing alone as an observation or as a comment on a given topic. Many sayings seem only loosely attached to their literary contexts, having little or nothing in common with those which come before or after. There are, however, some identifiable collectional features.

Although a connected train of thought cannot be traced through the whole of any chapter, there are occasions when it is possible to discern intentionality on the part of those who collected, arranged, or recorded these sayings in their present order. Some editorial groupings based on similarities in vocabulary or content can be found. For instance 10:2-5 all speak to the subject of wealth and poverty (in one way or another) while 10:18-21 all refer to the use of lips and tongue (speech).

Occasionally, we can discover clues to the opinions of the collectors. For instance if 18:11 is understood as an independent observation, with no relationship to its context, it seems to claim that wealth is able to protect its possessors (RSV "A rich man's wealth is his strong city, and like a high wall protecting him"). However, if 18:11 is read in conjunction with the verse which comes immediately before it ("The name of the LORD is a strong tower; the righteous man runs into it and is safe"), then the power of the claim made for wealth is greatly reduced. It is my opinion that the two sayings in 18:10-11 were deliberately placed next to each other. Intentionality on the part of those who handed the sayings on to us is a hermeneutical assumption (an interpretive perspective which I bring with me to the reading of these texts). I believe that whoever arranged these sayings in this order *intended* to give the comment about the rich in v. 11 a sarcastic tinge. In a similar way, it may be seen that juxtaposing 10:15 with 10:16 or 14:23 with 14:24 serves to reframe the meaning of the second saying in each pair. Such deliberate pairings of sayings can be seen as significant clues to the intentions of the collectors.

THE SECOND COLLECTION (25:1–29:27)

The first verse in ch. 25 acts as a title or a heading for what follows: "These also are proverbs of Solomon which the men of Hezekiah king of Judah copied." This collection resembles the first in some ways and differs from it in others. About half of the sayings preserved by Hezekiah's men follow the rigidly parallel "sentence proverb" format described above. But a number of sayings take two or three verses (four to six parallel phrases) for the completion of a single thought.

Some subjects (such as hypocrisy) occur more frequently and some subjects (such as righteousness) occur less frequently in the second section than they do in the first. Prohibitions and comparisons account for a much larger proportion of the sayings in the Hezekian collection than in its predecessor. There are many overlapping themes and a number of outright duplications. Chapter 29 in particular consists mostly of repetitions or variations of sayings found elsewhere.

In the first collection, editorial linkages account for the present order of only a small minority of verses. There is a great deal more discontinuity than order in the arrangement of the sayings in 10:1–22:16. But in the Hezekian collection quite a few distinct editorial groupings can be identified. The first seven verses in ch. 25 are on the topic of kingship, all but one of the sayings in 26:1-12 contain the word *kesil* ("fool"), the proverbs in 26:13-16 all refer to "sluggards," those in 26:17-26 deal with various misuses of the power of speech, and eight or more sayings in ch. 28 comment on the topic of poverty and riches.

The two collections are enough alike in form and content to justify our considering them together in this commentary. Since most of us find that reading long series of disconnected statements in the usual manner (chapter by chapter) is tedious and unproductive, the format of the commentary which follows will vary from the pattern used to discuss the longer poetic units in the first nine chapters.

After some general observations on literary styles and interpretive assumptions, we will attempt to discuss both collections of Solomonic sayings by subject matter rather than by chapters. Where appropriate, we will comment on editorial groupings and consider what light the collectional pairings might shed on the theological understandings of the collectors.

LITERARY STYLES AND INTERPRETIVE ASSUMPTIONS

The Nature of Popular or "Folk" Proverbs

Typical "folk" proverbs make pithy, apt observations about situations which tend to occur and recur in human experience. Their origins or authors are usually unknown and untraceable. They tend to circulate orally (by word of mouth). In most cases, proverbial sayings are more memorable for the way in which they express truth than for the truth itself. Thus, for instance, an English proverb such as "Birds of a feather flock together" is made memorable more by the sound of the phrase than by the distinctiveness of the idea it articulates. When proverbs are translated from one language to another, such features as assonance (the juxtapositioning of similar sounds) or wordplays (such as puns) are usually lost. Thus, the content of a proverb in translation (stripped of its striking or ear-catching language) may seem trite or insipid.

The truth expressed in proverbial sayings is usually understood to be particular (applicable only in certain situations) rather than universal (applicable in all conceivable situations), and the terms used in such sayings are often meant to be understood metaphorically rather than literally. Thus, those who quote a saying such as "A stitch in time saves nine" know that its "truth" applies to more than just mending and sewing and that "nine" is chosen more for its sound than for its invariable accuracy as a number. And usually those who say "You can lead a horse to water, but you can't make it drink" are using imagery drawn from animal husbandry to comment on an aspect of *human* nature.

It is clear from the biblical records that the people of Israel and Judah had folk proverbs such as these. For example, both Jeremiah and Ezekiel quote a saying commonly known to their contemporaries: "The fathers have eaten sour grapes, and the children's teeth are set on edge" (Jer. 31:29; Ezek. 18:2). But we have no way of knowing whether most (or if any) of the "Solomonic sayings" once had this type of popular currency.

LITERARY PROVERBS

Most interpreters think there is a higher degree of artificiality and more stylistic conformity in the Solomonic sayings than one would expect to find in a typical collection of folk proverbs. For instance Prov. 10:1–22:16 contains 375 sayings, and all but one of them consists of two parallel phrases (19:7, the sole exception, is a three-part saying). In the RSV (and in almost all other modern English translations) each half of a verse is made into a line of text, so that each verse consists of two parallel lines. Most of these sayings fall into one of three typical patterns of poetic expression (explained below). This would seem to be indicative of studied and knowledgeable composition rather than the results one would expect from popular coinage. The longer sayings that have been scattered throughout the Hezekian collection also seem more like carefully formulated poetry than "proverbs" in common usage.

However, scattered among the parallelisms in both Solomonic collections, we do find a few sayings which do not conform to any of the usual formal patterns. Some of these may have originated as folk proverbs which circulated orally among the common people. The imagery is often more striking and the forms of expression are more memorable in these variants than in the "typical" (or at least more numerous) parallelisms.

Several pairs of sayings have one of their two halves in common. Thus, for instance, both 10:15 and 18:11 begin with the statement "A rich man's wealth is his strong city," but their conclusions vary. This suggests the possibility that the phrase they share may have had an independent existence (as a folk proverb) before wisdom teachers or pupils added their different endings to it (cf. 17:3 and 27:21; 10:6 and 11).

A WORD IN SEASON

Whether or not the bulk of Solomonic sayings were deliberately composed by the "wise," whether or not they were widely circulated or known among the general populace, it is clear that these sayings do have a number of characteristics in common with the folk proverbs which occur in almost every human culture. Unlike laws or commandments which *advocate* certain types of behavior, many Solomonic sayings (like many folk proverbs) simply *describe* a type of human behavior which occurs often enough to be familiar to both the speaker and the listener. And unlike theological or philosophical statements, few of these sayings pretend to possess more than contextually limited truth.

Consider, for instance, a common English proverb like "Penny wise, pound foolish." In its own cultural context such a saying would never be understood as a command. It does not advise people to be careful of "pennies" and careless of "pounds." Those who quote such a saying are aware that the terms "penny" and "pound" can refer to things other than money. And they know intuitively that the proverb does not claim universality for the "truth" it contains. (It does not ask us to believe that every person who handles small amounts of money wisely is invariably short-sighted or deals unwisely with larger amounts.)

The same must be said for a proverb such as "A gracious woman gets honor, and violent men get riches" (11:16). Whether such a proverb is perceived as "true" when it is quoted depends upon whether it is used at precisely the right moment in exactly the right setting.

Simply being able to repeat a large number of proverbs does not make one wise. A proverb is useless and pointless in the mouth of a fool (26:7, 9). The wise are those who know how to choose and to use the right saying on the right occasion. A shrewd observer can make almost any proverb into a "true" statement by using it to comment upon the right occasion. It then becomes "a word in season" (15:23), expressing the truth of that particular situation in life (cf. 25:11).

Occasionally in the first collection and more often in the second section, a proverb will seem to advocate or to prohibit a certain course of action, (e.g., "Let your foot be seldom in your neighbor's house" 25:17). But even such prescriptive sayings must be carefully matched to fit appropriate settings. As John J. Collins notes, "The sage who tells you that 'he who hesitates is lost' will very probably also warn you to 'look before you leap.' Both pieces of advice are excellent, if you know when to apply them and when to disregard them" (*Proverbs, Ecclesiastes,* 13-14).

The sages of Israel can deliberately and knowingly list two completely opposite commands one right after the other, (e.g., in 26:4-5), because they know that there are times when it is wise to "answer a fool according to his folly" (v. 5) and times when it is wiser not to do so (v. 4).

DESCRIPTIVE VERSUS PRESCRIPTIVE TRUTHS

If we recognize the "seasonal" nature of many proverbial truths, then we will not be tempted to universalize such statements as "The poor is disliked even by his neighbor, but the rich has many friends" (14:20). This saying reflects upon an aspect of reality. It is an observation which may prove true in many human settings. But we ought not to assume that the speaker was asserting that all poor people everywhere are disliked by their neighbors.

Nor should we assume that either the person who coined the saying or the person who recorded it approved of the reality it describes. In oral usage, words and phrases in a proverb can take on different meanings through the intonations and gestures of the speaker. Ironic distance, disdain, and praise can all be communicated using the same words with different inflections. But if a proverb is known to us only in writing, it is difficult (if not impossible) to discover how its users might have felt about the statement it made.

However, in this particular case the reader can note that the saying in the following verse condemns the type of behavior described in 14:20: "He who despises his neighbor is a sinner, but happy is he who is kind to the poor" (v. 21). Whoever collected and listed these sayings in their present order had an opinion about the reality reflected in 14:20! In this example it can be seen that each saying expresses a complete thought. Each is capable of standing alone as a sense unit in its own right. But the fact that such sayings are listed right next to each other gives us a clue to the way the wise thought the Solomonic proverbs should be used. This juxtapositioning of verses should warn readers that the wise themselves were aware of the distance which separates observations from recommendations. Sayings which use evaluative terms such as "good" or "evil" and sayings which specify positive and negative consequences for particular behaviors have implicitly prescriptive powers. But those who want to be considered wise must learn to distinguish between sayings which comment on the way things *are* and statements which make claims about the way things *ought to be*. Only then can a "word" be said to be "fitly spoken" (25:11).

FIGURATIVE AND LITERAL SPEECH

When we are dealing with proverbs that originated in our own language and were popularized in our own culture, we usually know which terms can be understood literally and which have a figurative sense. In the midwestern United States "Bad apples fall near the tree" is never taken literally: its use invariably means that a child's misbehavior is being traced back to his or her parents. However, the interpretive task becomes more difficult when we are faced with sayings from a time, place, and culture far different than our own.

The literary context indicates that the people of Judah understood "grapes" and "teeth" (in "The fathers have eaten sour grapes, and the children's teeth are set on edge") as metaphorical. But it is much more difficult to determine whether references to eating in the sentence literature (such as "The LORD does not let the righteous go hungry" in 10:3) should also be seen as figurative rather than literal. Unfortunately, those who collected and arranged the sayings in 10:1–22:16 did not provide us with many contextual clues. Very little evidence can be found to argue conclusively for either the literal or the figurative understanding of such terms as "life," "death," "wealth," "hunger," and so forth.

However, the high proportion of metaphorical language found in the Instructions which now frame the Solomonic sayings suggests that at least some of the shorter sayings should also be read with figurative senses. In the Instructions eating and drinking often refer to more than the mere consumption of food and beverage. Thus, it is at least reasonable to suppose that both the "hunger" and the "craving" mentioned in 10:3 may have spiritual or psychological (rather than exclusively physical) applications. If so, its usage would parallel the traditional claim that human beings do not live "by bread alone" (Deut. 8:3).

The assumptions which interpreters bring with them to their task will, of course, affect their readings of the text. For instance, a footnote in the Oxford Annotated Bible indicates that the RSV has followed the LXX reading of Prov. 14:24a in rendering "the crown of the wise is their wisdom." However, the MT clearly reads "riches" in the place of "wisdom." If one understands "riches" in a literal sense, 14:24a sounds unpleasantly mercenary. Neither the LXX nor the RSV was willing to risk leaving the actual word "riches" in its respective translation. But a figurative reading of "riches" would give a non-materialistic sense to the original utterance, and both the LXX and RSV have communicated this non-literal sense to their audiences. For more on the literal or figurative understandings of life and death, see the Commentary under the topic heading "Matters of Life and Death" (pp. 78-80).

POETIC STRUCTURES

PARALLELISM

In Biblical Hebrew, poetry is distinguished from prose primarily by the presence or absence of parallel phrasing. Instead of rhyming sounds, Hebrew poets customarily "rhymed" ideas. The most common types of parallelism in the Solomonic sayings involve either synonymous or antithetical thought rhymes. Either the two halves of a verse state a single idea phrased in two slightly different ways (called synonymous parallelism), or two exactly opposite ideas are juxtaposed within the same sentence (called antithetical parallelism). A third and less frequently found technique (called synthetic or "stair-step" parallelism) involves adding ideas onto thoughts expressed in previous lines. Most of the sayings in chs. 10–15 are antithetical. Thus, the reader will note that "a wise son" in the first line of 10:1 is the opposite of "a foolish son" in the second line, and that "a glad father" is the antithesis of "a sorrow to his mother." But the sayings in chs. 16–22 are more varied. An excellent example of synonymous parallelism can be seen in 17:4. In this saying, "evildoer" has approximately the same meaning as "liar," while "listens to" is echoed by "gives heed to" and "wicked lips" corresponds with "mischievous tongue."

A saying such as 16:4 may be categorized as a synthetic parallelism, since its second line explains or expands upon the observation made in the first line.

COMPARISONS

A few of the Solomonic sayings can be characterized as comparisons or similitudes, which compare essentially unlike items in order to make an assertion about one of them. Thus, for example,

71

10:26 says that the way a lazy messenger affects those who send him is similar to the way vinegar affects the teeth, and smoke affects the eyes, while 25:13 compares a faithful messenger with the refreshing "cold of snow in the time of harvest." The collection made by Hezekiah's men has quite a few more similitudes than does the first Solomonic collection. Several editorial groupings of similitudes can be found, as in 25:12-14 or 26:7-11.

"BETTER" SAYINGS

One rather sophisticated type of saying takes the form "A with B is better than C with D," as in "Better is a dry morsel with quiet than a house full of feasting with strife" (17:1) or "Better is a dinner of herbs where love is than a fatted ox and hatred with it" (15:17). Seven of the sayings in the first Solomonic section follow this exact formula (12:9; 15:16-17; 16:8; 16:19; 17:1; 19:1), and one saying in the collection made by Hezekiah's men is very similar (28:6). Each of these "better sayings" is concerned with the hidden costs involved in making choices. Some desirable things come with undesirable conditions attached: some prices are too high to pay.

The mere presence of the word "better" does not automatically qualify a saying to fit into the "better saying" category. Two sayings in the Hezekian collection resemble the formula described above but lack the element of accompanying conditions. I would group "Better is open rebuke than hidden love" (27:5) and "Better is a neighbor who is near than a brother who is far away" (27:10b) with other sayings which use the words "better . . . than" to express what is essentially a preference for one thing over another (as in 16:32 or 22:1b).

TOPICS AND THEMES

THE RIGHTEOUS AND THE WICKED

Good and evil or righteousness and wickedness are the most frequently considered topics in the Solomonic sayings. References to righteousness *(tsedaqah)* and the righteous *(tsaddiq)*, which were seldom found in the Instructions in chs. 1–9, actually outnumber references to wisdom and the wise in 10:1–22:16. Similarly, words referring to evil *(ra')* and the wicked *(rasha')* occur far more often in the first Solomonic collection than words for fools and their folly. This emphasis on right and wrong, using terms which the prophets frequently cite as the basis for God's pleasure or displeasure, is particularly intense in chs. 10–13. If the present arrangement of chapters was intentional, then those who had a hand in the editorial process must have wanted the proverbs on righteousness and wickedness to set the tone for the reading of the whole first collection.

References to righteous(ness) and wicked(ness) occur much less frequently in the collection made by Hezekiah's men, and most of what is said on this topic is found in chs. 28 and 29. The majority of "righteousness" sayings in both collections speak primarily about the "fruits" or results of righteousness and wickedness. Thus, for example, it is said that "the LORD does not let the righteous go hungry" (10:3), that "the wicked are overthrown and are no more, but the house of the righteous will stand" (12:7), and that "misfortune pursues sinners, but prosperity rewards the righteous" (13:21). Righteousness, it is said, "delivers from death" (10:2; 11:4). Wickedness has the opposite result both on its owners (e.g., 13:6) and on their victims: "When the righteous are in authority, the people rejoice; but when the wicked rule, the people groan" (29:2).

73

However, only a few sayings indicate what kinds of actions are thought to fit into which category. We are told specifically that a righteous person "has regard for the life of his beast" (12:10), "hates falsehood" (13:5), and "gives and does not hold back" (21:26). A righteous person is also one who "knows the rights of the poor" (29:7).

In contrast, the wicked are said to be those who despise their neighbors (14:21), accept bribes in order to pervert justice (17:23), perpetrate violence (21:7), covet (21:26), have "haughty eyes and a proud heart" (21:4), and do not acknowledge the rights of the poor (29:7). The wicked seem to have guilty consciences: they "flee when no one pursues, but the righteous are bold as a lion" (28:1).

Other words which participate in the same semantic fields as righteousness include "uprightness" and the "upright" (as in 14:2; 11:3), "blameless" (as in 11:5), and "integrity" (as in 10:9). These words would be equally difficult to define simply on the basis of their occurrences in the sentence literature.

By implication we might conclude that actions which are praised or promised a reward can be equated with righteousness: since those who share their bread with the poor are said to be blessed (22:9), it is clear that they are considered upright. However, no words for righteousness or its synonyms are explicitly identified with this behavior. Again, only by implication, behavior which has negative consequences may be equated with evil: one whose wealth is increased by the oppression of the poor "will only come to want" (22:16) and may thus be judged to be in the wrong, as may those who refuse to hear the cry of the poor since they will themselves "cry out and not be heard" (21:13).

Apparently the speakers of proverbs relied upon other traditional sources to give content to their evaluative terms. Words such as "faithful," "righteous," and "upright," or "wicked," "sinful," and "evil" or their synonyms are used both in legal and in prophetic texts. We can only assume, on the basis of very limited evidence, that the wise used these traditional words in traditional ways. There is nothing in the book of Proverbs to indicate otherwise. If this is so, however, then the book takes on a much more ethical and religious orientation than most scholars have been willing to recognize within it.

Motives and Motivations

Actions alone are not the sole test of whether a person is righteous or wicked. The collectors of the sentence proverbs assert that the LORD judges intentions as well as deeds. Human "hearts" (the source of thoughts, inclinations, and will), "lie open before the LORD" (15:11), the LORD "weighs the heart" (21:2) and "tries [tests] hearts" for purity (17:3; cf. Jer. 17:9-10). You may think everything you do is right, but the LORD "weighs" the human "spirit" (Prov. 16:2) and uses it as a lamp to search our "innermost" thoughts (20:27; cf. 27:19).

Because the LORD always knows our intentions, the wicked do themselves no good by performing the outward forms of worship. "The sacrifice of the wicked is an abomination to the LORD" (15:8), especially when it is brought "with evil intent" (21:27). The wise echo 1 Sam. 15:22 when they assure their listeners that "to do righteousness and justice is more acceptable to the LORD than sacrifice" (Prov. 21:3).

Evil intentions (the wish to cause another harm) are thought to entrap the intender (26:27). However, intentions do not have to be entirely altruistic (i.e., without any benefit for the doer) in order to be judged "good." Thus, 25:21-22 follows its highly admirable-sounding advice ("If your enemy is hungry, give him bread to eat; and if he is thirsty, give him water to drink") with a self-serving motivational clause: "for you will heap coals of fire on his head, and the LORD will reward you" (cf. 24:17-18). The Egyptian sage Amenemope advises his listeners to "fill his [the wicked man's] belly with bread of thine, so that he may be sated and may be ashamed" (v.5; *ANET,* 422). Paul quotes Prov. 25:21-22 in its entirety, complete with its motivational clause (Rom. 12:20), but Jesus stands over against this aspect of wisdom when he asks his followers to love their enemies without expecting a reward (Matt. 5:43-46).

THE WISE AND THE FOOLISH

Wisdom and Knowledge

In the RSV the Hebrew word *hakam* is consistently translated "wise" and *hokmah* is translated "wisdom." As was the case with words denoting righteousness and wickedness, wisdom is more often praised than defined in the sentence proverbs. One speaker claims that a wise person can defeat "the mighty" (Prov. 21:22; cf. 24:5). We are also told however, that "the fear of the LORD is instruction in wisdom" (15:33) and that no wisdom "can avail against the LORD" (21:30). Wisdom is more likely to be found "with the humble" than with the proud or the insolent (11:2; 13:10). Those who wish to become wise must associate with the wise (13:20). However, wisdom may not be attainable for everyone (17:16).

Those who are wise will "heed commandments" and "keep the law" (10:8; 28:7), take advice (12:15; 13:1), and listen to "wholesome admonition" (15:31). Those who are "wise in their own eyes" are not considered wise at all (26:12; 28:26), an opinion which is shared by the Egyptian sage Ptah-hotep (*ANET*, 412). The wise act with caution (Prov. 14:16), speak judiciously (16:23), and avoid getting into arguments (e.g., 29:8, 11).

Wisdom is related to, but distinct from, knowledge (*da'at*). Those who are wise seek, acquire, and "lay up" knowledge (10:14; 18:15). But both knowledge and wisdom involve more than the mere ability to repeat information. The wise are those who know how to make effective use of what they have learned. They are able to apply their knowledge appropriately in concrete situations (14:8).

Prudence and Discernment

In addition to the basic word *hakam* and its derivatives, there is another family of words which seem to cover much of the same semantic range as wise does in English. The related words *binah, mebin, tebunah,* and *nabon* all derive from and participate in the meaning of *bin* ("discern" or "understand"), and can be translated in most cases with derivatives of those words (and their synonyms). Thus, *nabon* appears in the RSV as "understanding" in 14:6, 33; 15:14; 19:25; as "discernment" in 16:21; and as "intelligent" in 17:28; 18:15.

Again, we find that most of the words denoting various aspects of wisdom (which may have had different connotations in their original settings) seem interchangeable when they occur without a fixed context in the sentence proverbs. The RSV translates two entirely different Hebrew roots by the one English word "prudent." The "son who gathers in summer" in 10:5 is *maskil* ("prudent"), but the person who ignores an insult in 12:16 is *'arum* ("prudent"). In other OT usages, *'arum* seems to imply "cleverness" or "subtlety" (as in Gen. 3:1), and this connotation may still apply in Proverbs (e.g., it is opposed to the term "simple" in Prov. 14:15; 22:3). However, a person who knows when to keep quiet is called both *maskil* (in 10:19) and *'arum* (in 12:23), so the two words apparently do overlap in meaning.

Fools and Their Folly

In the Solomonic sayings the most commonly used term for "fool" is *kesil*, a word which is found only in the Psalms and in Wisdom literature. The *kesil* is improvident (Prov. 21:20), more interested in expressing an opinion than in understanding a subject (18:2), does not learn from punishment (17:10), "throws off restraint and is careless" (14:16), indulges in self-deception (my own translation of 14:8), hates to turn away from evil (13:19), and considers wrongdoing laughable (my translation of 10:23). The term *kesil* is used in eleven of the first twelve verses in ch. 26, which gives the reader a rather convenient way to examine the attitudes Hezekiah's men had toward fools and their folly.

The second most frequently used term for "fool" is *ewil*. We can deduce from the sayings that the *ewil* is one who does not "heed commandments" (10:8), will not listen to advice (12:15), "despises" parental instruction or discipline (15:5), and is quarrelsome (20:3). However, an *ewil* who keeps quiet may seem wise. The word *iwelet*, which the RSV translates as "folly," is derived from the same root as *ewil*. In 27:22 both *ewil* ("fool") and *iwelet* ("folly") are used in a saying which implies that folly is so thoroughly imbedded in a fool that it cannot be pressed or sifted out.

An English-speaking audience recognizes a root relationship between such English words as "fool," "foolish," "foolishness," and "folly." Thus, one who reads the RSV of 13:16b ("a fool flaunts his folly") might conclude that the translation echoes a double usage of the same root word in a single line of Hebrew text (as was the case in 27:22). But, in fact, in a number of cases the RSV fails to indicate that the Hebrew is using two entirely unrelated terms for "fool" and "folly." Thus, for instance, in 12:23;

13:16; 14:8, 24; 15:2, 14; 17:12 the translation "fool" is based on the Hebrew word *kesil,* while "folly" represents the word *iwelet.* Unfortunately, modern translators are not able to distinguish between the finer nuances of meaning which probably accompanied the different Hebrew words when they were first used to describe unwise forms of behavior. In addition to the frequently used *kesil* and *ewil,* the RSV translates still another word (*nabal,* which seems to connote emptiness or hollowness) by the same English term "fool" (17:7, 21).

Simpletons and the Senseless

The term *peti* (which occurs less frequently than *ewil* or *kesil*) is usually translated "the simple" in the RSV (as in 14:15, 18; 19:25; 21:11; 22:3). The simple seem to be those who are gullible or easily misled: "the simple believes everything" (14:15). The simple lack foresight, but they can learn from others' experiences— though not as easily as the "wise" or the "prudent" (19:25; 21:11). When prudent people see danger they hide from it, "but the simple go on, and suffer for it" (27:12).

A handful of sayings refer to someone who lacks a "mind" (*leb*). This idiom is translated as "lacks sense" in the RSV, "lacks judgment" in the NIV, and "void of understanding" in the KJV. Fools (*ewilim*) are said to "die for lack of sense" (10:21), and folly (*iwelet*) is said to be a joy to those without "sense" (15:21). Apparently, those who belittle their neighbors (11:12), follow worthless pursuits (12:11), and go into debt to their neighbors (17:18) are all thought by the wise to be lacking in mental equipment!

MATTERS OF LIFE AND DEATH

It is easier for the wise to say what *leads* to "life" than to say what life *is.* In the first section of Solomonic sayings, the teaching of the wise, reverence or "fear" of the LORD, and wisdom are all said to be "a fountain of life" (13:14; 14:27; 16:22). Both "a gentle tongue" and "the fruit of the righteous" are called "a tree of life" (15:4; 11:30). The fear of the LORD "prolongs life" (10:27) or "leads to life" (19:23), and "he who keeps the commandment keeps his life" (19:16). "The wage of the righteous leads to life" (10:16), guarding the way "preserves" life (16:17), those who "heed instruction" are "on the path to life" (10:17), and "the reward for humility and fear of the LORD is riches and honor and life" (22:4). The sayings copied by Hezekiah's men contain nothing resembling these statements about life. One who is "steadfast in righteousness will live," but one who "pursues evil will die" (11:19), as will one who "despises the word" (19:16; 13:13) or "hates reproof" (15:10). Death has "snares" (one of which is identified with the "getting of treasures by a lying tongue" (21:6), but these traps can be avoided through the teachings of the wise and through the fear of the LORD (13:14; 14:27). Fools, however, "die for lack of sense" (10:21). The "way of error leads to death" (12:28), some ways "seem right" and lead unexpectedly to death (14:12; 16:25), but "righteousness delivers from death" (10:2; 11:4). Again, Hezekiah's men apparently were not interested in sayings about death or dying.

There are also some more roundabout ways of talking about death and life in the sentence literature: "the lamp of the wicked will be put out" (13:9; cf. 24:20), the "years of the wicked will be short" (10:27), and one who "wanders from the way of understanding will rest in the assembly of the dead" (21:16).

We ought not to rule out the possibility that the word "life" is used in most of these sayings as a figure of speech referring to quality and quantity of life rather than to mere physical existence. Many interpreters think that "life" is used in proverbial statements to mean "a long and blessed life" and that "death" refers to an early demise (dying before one's time). Given the silence of most OT witnesses concerning the concepts of immortality or everlasting life, there is a high degree of probability that statements such as those about avoiding "the snares of death" (14:27; 16:22) meant simply avoiding a premature or tragic death rather than an escape from mortality itself.

However, a few interpreters think that some of the Solomonic sayings about life and death offer us glimpses into variant beliefs which were popularly held but were not a part of the received traditions (or the "official religion") of Israel. Most scholars think that nearly all OT references to Sheol portray it as a destination to which all the dead go, regardless of whether they had lived their lives in righteous or in wicked ways. Nevertheless, a few readers suggest that sayings such as 12:28; 15:24; or 20:20 reflect the idea that a different kind of afterlife might be available to those who live wisely and faithfully. Mitchell Dahood, for instance, has proposed that the second half of 12:28 should read "And the treading of her path [i.e., the path of righteousness] is immortality" ("Immortality in Proverbs 12:28," 179). There is, however, very little (if any) evidence to support Dahood's proposed emendation (see William McKane, *Proverbs,* 451). Again, a great deal depends on (a) the way the Hebrew is translated and (b) the preconceptions the interpreters bring with them to the text. For further discussion of the historical development of ideas about forms of retribution which are not restricted to this life, see below, pp. 203-6.

POVERTY AND PROSPERITY

Advantages and Disadvantages

Overall, the degree to which wealth is valued in the Solomonic sayings is surprisingly low. Possessions acquired through morally acceptable means (such as hard work and honest business dealings) are certainly thought to be desirable. But the protection of wealth is definitely not to be trusted: "riches do not profit in the day of wrath" (11:4), and "he who trusts in his riches will wither" (11:28). The hard work involved in attaining prosperity is thought by one or two observers to be of as much value to the person as the wealth itself (13:11; 20:21).

Choices made by translators contribute greatly to the average reader's understanding of the attitudes expressed by the wise in these chapters. For instance the RSV translates the second line in 11:7 as "the expectation of the godless comes to naught," while TEV reads "confidence placed in riches comes to nothing." In Hebrew the text is capable of being understood in either way. But the rendering of TEV allows the reader of the English text to see that 11:7 actually agrees with 11:28 and 11:4. Thus in TEV, three different statements in a single chapter observe that wealth is not an ultimately dependable form of protection. In a similar way, when a Hebrew word in 18:11 might be read either as "in his imagination" or "as his protection," the translators of the RSV have chosen the option which seems to claim that wealth really is a protecting wall around the rich, while contributors to TEV have concluded that rich people simply "imagine that their wealth protects them like high strong walls around a city." Since 18:11

immediately follows a declaration that the "name of the LORD is a strong tower" which protects the righteous, the option chosen by TEV is quite likely the one intended by those who originally placed these verses next to each other. The collector(s) probably used the grouping process intentionally as a way of commenting upon those who look to their wealth rather than to the LORD for "protection." It seems that the RSV has inadvertently obscured the irony which becomes clear when the two verses are read together as an intentional unit. If 18:11 is understood in the way I suggest it should be, it then becomes parallel to 28:11, which implies that the rich are mistakenly wise in their own eyes.

Another example of how translations can be misleading occurs in 13:8. In American usage the term "redemption" is usually understood in theological terms. But this is not at all the sense intended by the original. The words which the RSV translates "ransom" and "redemption" in 13:8 are synonymous in Hebrew. A person who is held for ransom is "redeemed" when the ransom money is paid. But even after the individual words are correctly interpreted, the intentions of the speaker remain ambiguous. It is unclear whether the second line in the saying should be understood as one of the advantages or as one of the disadvantages of being poor. On the one hand, the speaker may be saying simply that the rich have means to pay a ransom while the poor do not. On the other hand, the sage's point might be that the possession of wealth puts the rich in danger of being kidnapped while the poor are immune to such threats. TEV understands the words in this latter sense: "A rich man has to use his money to save his life, but no one threatens a poor man." A similar sort of ironic twist may be attributed to the observation that "wealth brings many new friends" (19:4). The speaker may be hinting that the possession of such friends could be considered one of the *dis*advantages of being rich.

The wise observe that the problems which come with being poor include being bereft of "friends" (14:20; 19:4, 7), having to be polite when the rich can get away with being rude (18:23), and being dominated by rich creditors (e.g., 22:7). But while it is better, on the whole, to be rich than poor, a number of things are said to be worse than poverty. It is better to be poor than to be a fool (12:9), a liar (19:22), or a hypocrite (19:1). It is better to be poor and walk in integrity than to be rich and perverse (28:6). A "good name" is more desirable than "riches" (22:1), and it is better to be content with only a few possessions than to have the kind of wealth that is gained through injustice or accompanied by strife and hatred (15:16-17; 16:8, 19; 17:1).

Such attitudes towards wealth and poverty cannot be said to be the exclusive possesion of Israel. According to the Egyptian vizier Ptah-hotep, "Wrongdoing has never brought its undertaking into port. (It may be that) it is fraud that gains riches, (but) the strength of justice is that it lasts. . . ." (*ANET*, 412). And Amenemope says, "Better is a measure that the god gives thee, than five thousand (taken) illegally" (viii.18), "Rejoice not thyself (over) riches (gained) by robbery, nor mourn because of poverty" (x.6), and "Better is bread, when the heart is happy, than riches with sorrow (ix.6 and xvi.12; *ANET*, 422-23).

Sources and Causes

The sayings concerned with the causes of poverty may be based on the assumption that each person has equality of opportunity and equal access to the resources of the land. If it is taken for granted that everyone has a plot of ground from which subsistence can be gained, then statements such as "a slack hand causes poverty" (10:4) or "an idle person will suffer hunger" (19:15) make sense of human experiences in such a setting. If equal starting points are presupposed, then love of sleep (20:13), love of pleasure (21:17), ignoring advice (13:18), and hasty planning (21:5) can all be blamed for an individual's failure to prosper. Everything else being equal, it may be observed that those who till the land will have "plenty of bread" while those who follow "worthless pursuits will have plenty of poverty" (28:19). However, the wise also recognize that greed and injustice on the part of the powerful can take away equality of opportunity: "The fallow ground of the poor yields [could yield] much food, but it is swept away through injustice" (13:23). In its present editorial context, 13:23 acts as a counterbalance to the opinions expressed in the two preceding verses. Through the editorial juxtapositioning of opposites, the wise remind their readers that neither of the strictly retributive sayings in 13:21-22 should be understood as statements of absolute or categorical truth.

In a similar vein, various sayings recognize that riches can be gained in different ways, through diligence and hard work (10:4; 12:27; 21:5), through alertness and foresight (20:13), as well as through injustice (28:20), "by interest and increase" (28:8), through miserliness (28:22), or through morally questionable practices (13:11; 21:6). Again it may be necessary to remind those who read these sentences that proverbial utterances are not usually meant to be universalized. Typically, each encapsulates and articulates an aspect of reality which can be recognized as true only when it is applied to an appropriate setting. It is the never-ending task of the "wise" to analyze whatever situations in life they encounter and to try to determine what is true in any given case. It is not necessary to deny the fact that injustice has been a source of wealth in some situations (22:16) in order to affirm that some riches are experienced as "blessings" given by God (e.g., 22:4). Since circumstances differ, no single saying can hold true in every human setting.

Self-Serving Humanitarianism

Most of the sayings which encourage humanitarian behavior do so for basically self-serving ends: those who are kind are said to benefit themselves (11:17), those who are generous grow prosperous (11:25), and those who share their bread with the poor "will be blessed" (22:9) and "will not want" (28:27). On the one hand, those who are "kind to the poor" are said to "lend to the LORD," and the LORD is expected to repay them (19:17). On the other hand, those who close their ears "to the cry of the poor" will themselves "cry out and not be heard" (21:13), and those who hide their eyes "will get many a curse (28:27). The collection of sayings which begins in 10:1 ends with a warning that those who oppress the poor to increase their own wealth "will only come to want" (22:16).

Only a few of the proverbs explicitly link the LORD's name with the promotion of social justice. In addition to "The LORD tears down the house of the proud, but maintains the widow's boundaries" (15:25), there are several denunciations of false scales and measures (11:1; 20:10, 23; cf. 16:11). However, the human dignity and worth of the poor are referred to by their status in relationship to God. "The LORD gives light to the eyes" of both the poor and those who oppress them (29:13). The LORD is the "maker" of both rich and poor (22:2), and both those who "mock" and those who "oppress" the poor are said to "insult" their "Maker" (17:5a; 14:31a). The wise believe that those who rejoice in the poverty of others "will not go unpunished" (17:5b) and that those who are "kind" to the needy "honor" God (14:31b). Finally, we should note that in ch. 28 (where a series of statements about the rich and the poor have been combined) it is said that the poor who oppress the poor are like "a beating rain that leaves no food" (28:3). The rain is ordinarily expected to be a blessing, and the poor would ordinarily expect empathy and support from those who share in their poverty. A reversal in our expectations is both shocking and devastating. Amenemope shares this opinion with his Israelite counterparts: "God desires respect for the poor more than the honoring of the exalted" (xxvi.12; *ANET,* 424).

THE POWER OF SPEECH

A number of sayings (including several editorial clusters) are concerned with wise and foolish ways of using human powers of communication. Fully, a third of the sayings in chs. 10, 12, and 26 are related to this topic. The sayings acknowledge that "death and life are in the power of the tongue" (18:21), that "a soft tongue will break a bone" (25:15), that "the lips of the wise will preserve them" (14:3), and that the speech of the "worthless" is "like a scorching fire" (16:27). Thus, the originators of these sayings endorse a viewpoint shared by many of their counterparts in other cultures. For instance in the Instruction of Ani an Egyptian sage says, "A man may fall to ruin because of his tongue" (vii.7-11; *ANET,* 420), and in the Elephantine texts the Assyrian scribe Ahiqar says, "More than all watchfulness watch thy mouth. . . . For a word is a bird: once released no man can recapture it," and "Soft is the tongue of a king, but it breaks a dragon's ribs" (The Words of Ahiqar vii.98, 105b-106; *ANET,* 428-29). This same attitude is echoed in a later era by a NT author: "The tongue is a little member and boasts of great things. How great a forest is set ablaze by a small [tongue of] fire!" (Jas. 3:5-8).

In societies based on oral rather than written tradition, it is the tongue rather than the pen which is "mightier than the sword." The Egyptian king Merikare's father says, "the tongue is a sword . . . and speech is more valorous than any fighting" (*ANET,* 415). The wise in Israel acknowledge that people can be wounded or healed (Prov. 12:18; 25:15), destroyed or delivered (11:9), stirred up or calmed down (15:1) by words. Many of the sayings assert that the proper and improper uses of speech have predictable results and that human beings have to live with the consequences of what they say (e.g., 12:13-14; 18:20-21).

When fools talk, they "advertise their ignorance" (12:23 TEV) and expose themselves to ridicule and danger (14:3; 18:6-7). After all, the more you talk the more likely you are to make a mistake (10:19), and even fools can appear to be wise if they keep their mouths shut (17:27-28). Thus, prudence consistently teaches the wise to be careful of what they say (13:3; 21:23), to think before they speak (15:28; 16:23; 18:13), and to keep quiet as much as possible (11:12; 12:23).

The names for body parts connected with speech are used more frequently in Proverbs than generic terms such as "talking" or "speaking." We often do the same in English, and thus we can easily understand the metaphorical references of statements such as "A gentle tongue is a tree of life" (15:4). Taken as a literal and categorical statement, a saying such as "Truthful lips endure for ever, but a lying tongue is but for a moment" (12:19) might seem like wishful thinking on the part of the speaker. But as a metaphor concerned with the purposes of God, it has the force of a faith claim.

Faithful and Unfaithful Communications

Both words and body language can be used as forms of communication (10:10; 16:30), but only speech that is open and above-board without pretense is said to be righteous and wise (26:23-26). By definition those who are righteous speak wisdom and those who are wicked do not (10:31-32). People's characters are judged by what they say (15:28; 17:7).

It may be human nature to relish "tasty" morsels of gossip (as TEV translates 18:8, duplicated in 26:22), but the wise know enough to avoid "talebearers" (11:13), "whisperers" (16:28), and spreaders of "slander" (10:18). Quarrels are precipitated by "whisperers" (26:20), and "a backbiting tongue" brings forth "angry looks" (25:23). Disclosing another's secret is to be avoided, because it may "bring shame upon you" (25:9-10). Only evildoers listen to "wicked lips," and only liars give heed to "a mischievous tongue" (17:4). Those who "belittle" their neighbors "lack sense" (11:12), and whoever "utters slander" is a fool (10:18).

On the other side of slander, flattery is also a perversion of truth. The wise must avoid either giving or being taken in by flattery. In the collection made by Hezekiah's men, "honey" is used as a metaphor for flattery: it is sweet, but swallowing too much of it is not healthy (25:27; cf. v. 16; 27:7). "A man who flatters his neighbor spreads a net for his feet" (29:5), and "a flattering mouth works ruin" (26:28).

Lying is of course a blatant misuse of the powers of speech. "A lying tongue hates its victims" (26:28). Any "treasures" gained by lying will soon vanish (21:6), and a person who lies and then says, "I am only joking," is likened to a "madman who throws firebrands" (26:18-19).

The editorial grouping in 12:13-22 links the telling of truth or lies to the success or failure of the judicial system. Those who speak the truth enable justice to be done in the courts and in the gates, but false witnesses clearly pervert the process. Seeing this essential link with justice enables us to put "Lying lips are an abomination to the LORD, but those who act faithfully are his delight" (12:22) in its proper context. According to both 19:5 and 9, "a false witness will not go unpunished," and those who utter lies in court will "perish" (v. 9) and "not escape" (v. 5).

JUSTICE AND COURTROOM ETHICS

The topic of justice is closely related to that of speech. Both civil and criminal cases were argued before the elders (respected members of the community) who met "in the gate" (an area specially designed for this purpose was built into the entryways of fortified cities). Anyone having knowledge of the case was publicly charged (under penalty of a curse) to come forward and testify (Lev. 5:1). Thus, it may be said that an accomplice (or even one who has knowledge of a crime but does not come forward to testify) "hates his own life; he hears the curse, but discloses nothing" (Prov. 29:24).

Perjury (giving a false testimony) under such a system brings about a failure in justice: "A worthless witness mocks at justice" (19:28). The story in 1 Kgs. 21 (about Naboth's vineyard) illustrates the lethal power lying witnesses can have. The saying that attributes the power of life and death to the tongue (Prov. 18:21) may be most appropriately quoted in this legal setting. The wise threaten those who give false witness with certain punishment (19:5, 9), assuming (perhaps) but not specifying that such punishment will come from the hand of God. The speaker in the Egyptian Instruction of Amenemope says "God hates him who falsifies words" (xiv.2; *ANET*, 423).

Justice can also be subverted by corruption and the acceptance of bribes on the part of the decision makers (Prov. 17:23). In any case, it is hoped that one who "sows injustice will reap calamity" (22:8).

One sage observes that the person who states his (or her) case first "seems right, until the other comes and examines him" (18:17). Occasionally, it is not possible for human judges to decide on the merits of a case. Then "the lot puts an end to disputes and decides between powerful contenders" (18:18). When lots are cast, the decision is no longer in human hands, but "wholly from the LORD" (16:33; cf. 1 Sam. 14:41-42). The wisdom of experience advises others not to enter too hastily into legal disputes. It is always possible that you yourself will be put to shame in the process (Prov. 25:8).

The wise believe that justifying the wicked and condemning the righteous are "both alike an abomination to the LORD" (17:15). To praise the wicked is the same as forsaking the law (28:4). Only those who "seek the LORD" understand justice completely (28:5). "It is not good to be partial" to the wicked or to deprive the righteous person of justice (18:5). However, the wise have observed human nature enough to know full well that even a strong man will do wrong "for a piece of bread" (28:21). Thus, "when justice is done, it is a joy to the righteous" and "dismay to evildoers" (21:15). In the final analysis it has to be said that "from the LORD a man gets justice" (29:26). Furthermore, the wise are convinced that those who escape the punishment they deserve from the human courts will be subject to other forms of chastisement. The saying in 28:17 may reflect this attitude towards those who seem to "get away with murder."

In translation, deprived of its original appeal to the listener's ear, "To impose a fine on a righteous man is not good; to flog noble men is wrong" (17:26) may sound hackneyed. But its content is not as trivial as its translation makes it seem. If it were used proverbially to comment appropriately upon an actual situation in life, it would not seem trite. The same might be said of 18:5.

Bribes

The Solomonic sayings do not condemn bribes per se. Gifts and bribes are equated in 21:14, and words meaning "gift" seem to be used interchangeably with words meaning "bribe" throughout the sentence literature. On the one hand, the speakers observe and describe (rather than advocate) what they know to be a reality in human communities: judiciously given "gifts" can open up new opportunities (as in 18:16) and defuse potentially dangerous situations (as in 21:14). On the other hand, they do not consider all bribes equal. Bribes which are given or taken to "pervert the ways of justice" are said to be evil (17:23). However, people who avoid taking the kinds of bribes which lead to "unjust gain" are said to "live" (15:27).

The RSV translation of 17:8 tends to obscure any possible distance between what the observer thinks and what the giver of bribes thinks. But, in fact, the speaker does not ask us to believe that the giving of bribes *will* guarantee anyone's prosperity. He or she merely observes that people who give bribes *think* this will be the result of their actions. TEV more accurately captures the irony inherent in the saying: "Some people think a bribe works like magic; they believe it can do anything." In a similar way, the speaker who observes that "every one is a friend to a man who gives gifts" (19:6) may be speaking with tongue in cheek, expecting the audience to recognize the irony implicit in the situation described.

ADVICE AND CORRECTION

The originators of the sentence proverbs seem to agree with the teacher in the third Instruction who said, "Be not wise in your own eyes" (3:7; cf. 26:12). The voice of experience says, "Listen to advice and accept instruction, that you may gain wisdom for the future" (19:20). The wisdom of many is seen to be superior to the wisdom of one. Those who trust in their own minds alone are foolish (28:26). "Without counsel plans go wrong, but with many advisers they succeed" (15:22), and "in an abundance of counselors there is safety" (11:14).

Sensible people give weight to the experiences of others: they value other people's opinions. Opinions that are given or solicited before any action is taken are usually called "advice" or "counsel" (as in 13:10 or 20:18). Opinions that are given after the fact (and disagree with the actions taken) may be called "rebuke" or "correction." In English, the meaning of "instruction" can overlap with the meanings of both advice and correction.

Several Hebrew words which refer to the way one person comments on another person's behavior seem nearly synonymous. We cannot recover their original nuances from the ways they are used in the sentence literature. The RSV is fairly consistent in translating *musar* as either "discipline" or "instruction," as distinct from *tokahat* ("reproof"), as in 12:1 or 13:18. However, in 16:22 "folly" is said to be the "chastisement" *(musar)* of fools. Usually, the sayings seem to have oral forms of correction in mind. But in 13:24 it is clear that the speaker uses *musar* as a synonym for corporal punishment (as also in 22:15; 29:19; and 1 Kgs. 12:11). In Egyptian school texts, the word for "instruction" also means "reproof" and "flogging," and it is quite possible that the Hebrew speakers in Proverbs held this understanding of education in common with their Egyptian counterparts (Nil Shupak, "The 'Sitz im Leben' of the Book of Proverbs," 109).

The proverbs observe that the wise are willing to listen to and learn from advice, instruction, correction, and rebuke. Those who ignore *musar* hurt (RSV "despise") themselves (15:32), while those who heed it gain "understanding" (literally, a heart/mind). Those who are "stiff-necked" (who stubbornly persist in ignoring correction) "will suddenly be broken beyond healing" (29:1). In the long run, says one speaker, those who give rebukes when they are needed will "find more favor" than those who flatter (28:23).

"The fear of the LORD" itself is equated with "instruction in wisdom" (15:33), and one who "heeds" *musar* "is on the path to life" (10:17). In the Instructions the wisdom teacher says, "My son, do not despise the LORD's discipline *(musar)* or be weary of his reproof *(tokahat),* for the LORD reproves him whom he loves, as a father the son in whom he delights" (3:11-12). The Solomonic sayings share this opinion that discipline and correction are a part of love (13:24; 19:18) and, in return, the child who is disciplined "will give delight to your heart" (29:17).

References to the "rod" of discipline (13:24; 22:15; 29:15)

were probably understood literally, in terms of corporal punishment. Several sayings refer to beatings which fools call down upon themselves, reflecting cultural assumptions or aspects of the speakers' society which some readers may find offensive. Again, we need to remember that proverbs often describe reality as it was observed by the speaker. After studying the school texts of ancient Egypt, Nil Shupak observes that "a customary approach to speeding up the process of learning in ancient schools was the threat or actual administration of floggings" (p. 109). A comparable saying is found in the Words of Ahiqar: "Withold not thy son from the rod, else thou wilt not be able to save him from wickedness" (vi.81; *ANET,* 428).

The Israelites clearly shared this culturally conditioned attitude with their counterparts in the rest of Mesopotamia. However, it is also true that a *shebet* (translated "rod," "staff," or "scepter") can be seen as a symbol of authority as well as an instrument of punishment. And in the hand of a good (wise?) shepherd, a "rod" can be a comforting, rather than a threatening object (Ps. 23:4). See also the Commentary on Prov. 23:13-14 in the "Sayings of the Wise" section of Proverbs.

ANGER AND ARGUMENTS

When speech is misused it can stir up anger (15:1) and start arguments (18:6), but good sense, wisdom, and understanding make a person "slow to anger" and reluctant to enter into a quarrel (14:29; 15:18; 19:11; 20:3). It is said to be as foolish to meddle in someone else's quarrel as it is to take "a passing dog by the ears" (26:17). The wise observe that an argument, once started, is difficult to stop. So they advise their listeners to "quit before the quarrel breaks out" (17:14), to "keep aloof from strife" (20:3), and to "overlook an offense" (19:11). "Hatred stirs up strife, but love covers all offenses" (10:12), and the wise "turn away wrath" (29:8).

A hot temper is considered a serious character flaw. Anger can be habit-forming (19:19), and people with quick tempers act foolishly and stir up strife (14:17, 29; 15:18; 26:21; 29:22). Only fools give "full vent" to their anger: the wise person "quietly holds it back" (29:11). As bad as anger is, however, jealousy is worse (27:4).

Patience and self-control, on the other hand, are virtues (14:17). Patience is worth more than a ruler's power. As TEV says, "It is better to win control over yourself than over whole cities" (16:32). Conversely, a person without self-control "is like a city broken into and left without walls" (25:28).

KINGSHIP AND POLITICS

Our understanding of the kingship proverbs is limited by our inability to recover the actual contexts in which the sayings might have been used. Thus, for instance, "Without people a prince is ruined" (14:28b) or "By justice a king gives stability to the land, but one who exacts gifts ruins it" (29:4; cf. 28:16) could serve equally well as advice directed either to the king himself or to his dissatisfied subjects (so also 20:28; 29:12, 14). Similarly, 21:1 might have been used to commend the rightness of the king's decisions, or it might have been used to remind the king that God's power was greater than his own. "A king who sits on the throne of judgment winnows all evil with his eyes" (20:8) may have been understood as either a positive or a negative comment on a ruler's ability to make good judgments (cf. 20:26).

In the editorial grouping consisting of 16:12-15, we find two sayings reflecting reality as it has been experienced by the speakers (i.e., they have discovered that it is wise to keep someone as powerful as the king happy; vv. 14-15). These observations are echoed in 19:12; 20:2, which both draw an analogy between an angry king and a hungry lion (cf. 28:15, where "a wicked ruler over a poor people" is said to be like "a roaring lion or a charging bear"). However, the speakers in 16:12-13 either have had different experiences with rulers and kings or they are reflecting their ideals (what they think kings should be like), rather than their actual experiences (cf. 22:11). Perhaps 16:14-15 were placed here as a deliberate contrast to the sentiments expressed in vv. 12-13. In their present grouping, the second pair of sayings serves as a warning to those who would actually try (on the basis of what is said in vv. 12-13) to speak "what is right" to the king. As a whole, this editorial cluster in ch. 16 says that while it may sometimes be true that the king wants an honest answer, those who are wise should remain fully aware that royal wrath is deadly.

The kingship saying in 16:10 could be taken at face value, as a straightforward statement of belief in a king's ability to speak with divine authority. But it might also have been said with tongue in cheek, as a warning against rousing the king's ire by questioning his judgments. Given the reality of the king's power, one might as well treat the king's pronouncements as though they were inspired!

Another editorial grouping is found in 25:2-7, where three sayings (each consisting of two verses) comment upon aspects of kingship. The first and third sayings seem to be addressed to those who need to know how to act in the presence of the king. Thus, the saying in vv. 2-3 seems to imply that it is quite proper for kings to search out answers but improper for anyone else to try to get an answer from the king. The third saying in this cluster (vv. 6-7) advises modesty on the part of those who come into the king's presence, "for it is better to be told 'Come up here,' than to be put lower in the presence of the prince." Similar advice is given in the Instruction of the Vizier Ptah-hotep (120; *ANET*, 412).

However, the second saying (Prov. 25:4-5) is concerned not with court etiquette but with the characteristics of a good king. The speaker here asserts (in language reminiscent of Isa. 9:7; 16:5) that the wicked need to be removed from the presence of the king, so that "his throne will be established in righteousness" (cf. duplications of this phrase in Prov. 16:12; 29:14). Since Isaiah undoubtedly lived and preached during the reign of Hezekiah, it is interesting to note resemblances between what Isaiah expected and what the proverbs copied by Hezekiah's men said the king should be like. The Hezekian collection seems to expect kings to live up to quite a high standard. Hezekiah's scribes tie the stability of the land directly to the wisdom and the righteousness of its ruler (28:2, 16; 29:4, 12, 14). A kingship saying in the first Solomonic section also may be related to this view of the king's responsibilities. In 20:28 "loyalty and faithfulness preserve the king" could refer to the king's loyalty and faithfulness as God's representative rather than to the loyalty and faithfulness of the king's subjects to his rule. If so, then this saying also puts the burden of responsibility for the stability of the throne onto the king's own shoulders.

This high view of what kingship ought to do for a land or a people was not unique to Israel or Judah. Many nations in the ancient Near East cherished similar ideals. The famous law code of Hammurabi, the sixth king of the Old Babylonian Dynasty (17th cent. B.C.E.), says that the king was commissioned by the gods to establish justice in the land and to promote the welfare of the people he governed (*ANET,* 165). An Egyptian document from the end of the 22nd cent. (addressed by an unnamed king to his son Meri-ka-re) advises the king to "do justice" and to avoid oppressing the "widow," removing boundary markers, or punishing the innocent (*ANET,* 415).

Although the word "king" is not mentioned in Prov. 17:2, the clever "slave" (or "servant," since Hebrew *ebed* can be understood either way) who comes to rule over the "son who acts shamefully" may easily be understood to be the king's servant (cf. 14:35; 29:21).

Although 27:23-27 seems on the surface to be concerned only with animal husbandry, v. 24 hints that its message may be addressed to a king or to a potential ruler (cf. Ezek. 34). The listener is advised to keep an eye on the condition of the "flocks" which are the source of his wealth, because "riches do not last for ever," and a "crown" may not always endure. On the one hand, this little section might be taken as nothing more than prudent agricultural advice. On the other hand, it might be wisely coded counsel concerning prudent political maneuvers.

BUSINESS DEALINGS

Four of the Solomonic sayings make virtually the same claim: the LORD favors equity and fairness in human commerce. Cheating the customer through dishonest scales, weights, or measures is "an abomination to the LORD" (11:1; 16:11; 20:10, 23). Several Egyptian wisdom sayings advocate a similar point of view. For example, the Instruction of Amenemope advises: "Do not lean on the scales nor falsify the weights. . . . Make not for thyself weights which are deficient; They abound in grief through the will of god" (*ANET,* 423).

One straightforward and intentionally humorous observation about the reality of buying and selling in ancient times still rings true in our own time: in the seller's presence, buyers moan that the price is too high, only later to boast of the bargains they got (Prov. 20:14).

One saying comments on what some merchants might think of as "good business" in hard times: the people curse one who "holds back grain" (waiting, perhaps, for higher prices in a time of famine?), but "a blessing is on the head" of the one who sells it when the people need it (11:26).

Debt

The attitude towards debt which characterized the wisdom instructor in 6:1-5 prevails here in the sayings material as well. "The borrower is the slave of the lender" (22:7), and only someone "without sense gives a pledge, and becomes surety" (17:18). The terms "surety" and "pledge" used by the RSV in 11:15; 17:18; and 20:16 have fallen out of common usage. TEV captures their meanings in modern terms: "Anyone stupid enough to promise to be responsible for a stranger's debts ought to have his own property held to guarantee payment" (20:16). The sayings in 20:16 and 27:13 are identical.

The legal codes which are considered a part of Israel's covenant with the LORD contain numerous regulations concerning borrowing and lending (e.g., Deut. 24:10-13). Within the covenant community, Israelites were forbidden to exact interest on a loan (cf. Deut. 23:19). Thus, one of the Hezekian sayings warns those who augment their wealth "by interest and increase" that what they earn will be taken from them and given to those who are more charitable towards the poor (Prov. 28:8).

FAMILY AND FRIENDS

The first Solomonic sayings collection begins in 10:1 with an observation which is repeated (with slight variations) in 15:20; 17:21, 25; and 19:13a. On the one hand, the sayings note that parents are blessed by the wisdom and righteousness of their children (10:1a; 15:20a; 27:11; 29:3) and that children are blessed if they have parents who behave wisely (20:7). Children can be as proud of their parents as grandparents are of their grandchildren (17:6). On the other hand, children who act foolishly bring grief, ruin, and shame upon their parents (10:1b; 17:21, 25; 19:13a; 28:7). The wise see disgrace and shame heaped upon children who mistreat their parents (19:26; 28:24) and warn that dire consequences are in store for those who "curse" them (20:20). See also Agur's comment in 30:17.

"Brothers" and Neighbors

The word translated "brother(s)" can also mean "kinfolk" or "relatives" in a more general sense. One saying which refers to relatives is unintelligible (18:19). Two others rate the loyalty expected from a "brother" fairly high, though not higher than one might expect from a true friend (17:17; 18:24). However, some speakers cast a more cynical eye over human relationships. One sage says, "Do not go to your brother's house in the day of your calamity" (27:10), and another observes, "All a poor man's brothers [relatives] hate him" (19:7). Some are inclined to think that friends (or neighbors) are not much more reliable than kin (19:4, 6-7). In a pinch, however, a nearby neighbor is better than a distant "brother," particularly if the neighbors are longtime family friends (27:10).

Some advice for keeping the friends you have: do not bless your neighbor in a loud voice very early in the morning (27:14), do not keep bringing up old offenses (17:9), and "let your foot be seldom in your neighbor's house" (25:17).

Women and Wives

In Hebrew the word *ishshah* can mean either "woman" or "wife." Translators use the contexts in which the word occurs to help them decide which English word best expresses the speaker's intentions. The RSV uses "woman" in 11:16; 11:22; 21:9, 19; 27:15 and "wife" in 12:4; 18:22; 19:13-14. The sayings in the first Solomonic collection are about evenly divided into positive and negative reflections. On the one hand, the speakers observe that "he who finds a wife finds a good thing, and obtains favor from the LORD" (18:22). Similarly, a "prudent" woman or wife (the word translated "prudent" is also translated "wise" in other verses) is said to be a gift from the LORD (19:14). On the other hand, those who feel less blessed in their marriages note that "a wife's quarreling is a continual dripping of rain" (19:13) and that it is better to live "in a corner of the housetop" or "in a desert land" than with a "contentious woman" (21:9, 19; 25:24). It is impossible to tell whether the unflattering simile in 11:22 refers simply to any woman without discretion or specifically to a wife without discretion.

The sayings copied by Hezekiah's men contain only two statements about women, and both repeat negative observations made in the first collection of sayings (25:24 repeats 21:9, and 27:15 is an adaptation of 19:13).

The meaning of 11:16 is something of an enigma. The RSV translates, "A gracious woman gets honor, and violent men get riches," while the NIV is more palatable: "A kindhearted woman gains respect, but ruthless men gain only wealth." The meaning of the Hebrew is unclear.

A close look at 12:4 indicates once again that the assumptions translators bring with them from their own cultural backgrounds inevitably affect their translations. Here the adjective which modifies "wife" in 12:4 is translated "good," in the RSV, so that the first line of this verse reads, "A good wife is the crown of her husband." But when the Hebrew adjective *(hayil)* occurs elsewhere in the OT, it is usually understood to mean "strong" (as in 2 Kgs. 2:16) or "able" (as in 1 Chr. 26:7-9). The NIV translates the phrase "a wife of noble character," while the NEB and NJV choose "a capable wife." See the related discussion on the woman who is said to be *hayil* in the concluding poem in Prov. 31:10-31.

The RSV also leaves out a Hebrew reference to women in 14:1, translating "Wisdom builds her house" rather than a more literal rendition, "the wisdom of women builds her house" (author's version) or "the wisest of women builds her house" (NJV) or "every wise woman buildeth her house" (KJV).

Since the Instructions in chs. 1–9 contained so many warnings against liaisons with "foreign women," it is somewhat surprising to find that this term occurs only once in the entire Solomonic sayings section. In 22:14 where the Hebrew literally says "The mouth of *zarot* ['foreigners,' feminine plural] is a deep pit," the RSV translates the term as "loose woman."

Adultery is not specifically mentioned in any of the Solomonic sayings. The only other possible reference to the popular instructional topic of sexual infidelity may be in 27:8; but if this is indeed its meaning, it is couched in very delicate terms: "Like a bird that strays from its nest, is a man who strays from his home."

PLANNING, FORESIGHT, AND THE WILL OF GOD

Those who are wise plan ahead: they try to foresee the consequences of their actions (14:15; 21:5). Two identical sayings (one in each of the two collections) compare the "prudent" who see danger coming and hide from it with the "simple" who are oblivious to danger signals and thus walk right into trouble (22:3; 27:12). But the wise also see that we cannot really know "what a day may bring forth" (27:1). "It is the glory of God to conceal things" (25:2), and God's plans always take precedence over human plans. God always has the last word. No matter what human beings plan to do, "it is the purpose of the LORD that will be established" (19:21; cf. 16:1, 3, 9, 33). A pair of sayings at the end of ch. 21 encapsulates the typical outlook expressed in the sentence proverbs: "No wisdom, no understanding, no counsel, can avail against the LORD. The horse is made ready for the day of battle, but the victory belongs to the LORD" (21:30-31).

"DILIGENCE" AND "SLOTH"

The RSV uses terms which have become archaic in our time. However, hard work is still glorified and laziness is still condemned as often in modern industrial societies as it was among the wise in Israel. Some of the Solomonic sayings have agricultural foundations: laziness is equated with sleeping in harvest time (10:5) and failing to plow in the right season (20:4). Those who till the land "will have plenty of bread" (12:11; 28:19), but "an idle person will suffer hunger" (19:15; 28:19).

Other sayings have more generalized references: "The hand of the diligent will rule, while the slothful will be put to forced labor" (12:24). The lazy are said to have unfulfilled cravings, while the diligent do not (13:4; cf. 12:27), and they are said to be wiser in their own eyes than "seven [people] who can answer discreetly" (26:16). The "sluggard" is satirized as one who turns in bed "as a door turns on its hinges" (26:14) and as one who gives ridiculous reasons for staying at home ("There is a lion in the streets!" 26:13; 22:13). Some are even said to be too lazy to lift food from the dish to their mouths (19:24; 26:15). Sending a lazy person on an errand is said to be as irritating to the wise as smoke to the eyes or vinegar to the teeth (10:26), and those who are slack in their work are considered as undesirable as those who are destructive (18:9). In Ecclesiastes the proverbial attitude towards work will be held up for examination. We will see that Ecclesiastes does not encourage laziness, but that the speaker does challenge people to evaluate the goals or the purposes which motivate them to work the hardest.

HUMILITY AND PRIDE

According to the Solomonic proverbs, pride (meaning arrogance or haughtiness) breeds quarrels (13:10), leads to disgrace (11:2), and is followed by destruction (16:18; 18:12). It is said that "the LORD tears down the house of the proud" (15:25) and that those who are arrogant are "an abomination to the LORD" (16:5). Several Hebrew words express very similar concepts. We cannot always tell from the translations whether different words are being used or not. In the RSV a single word in Hebrew is translated "pride" in 11:2 and "insolence" in 13:10. Another word becomes "arrogant" in 16:5 and "haughty" in 16:18, while two entirely different words lie beneath the "haughty" and "proud" of 21:4.

The proud, haughty person who acts with arrogant pride is also called a "scoffer" (21:24). Scoffers do not like to be reproved (13:1; 15:12), are not able to acquire wisdom (14:6), and are the source of strife, quarreling, and abuse (22:10). In direct contrast we are told that "with the humble is wisdom" (11:2) and that "humility goes before honor" (15:33; 18:12). The wise are advised, "Let another person praise you, and not your own mouth" (27:2). A person who is "lowly in spirit will obtain honor" (29:23).

In 15:33 humility is equated with "the fear of the LORD," and in 22:4 it is claimed that "the reward for humility and fear of the LORD is riches and honor and life."

JOY AND SORROW

The wise offer us their observations based on experience. On the one hand, the wise observe that "a glad heart makes a cheerful countenance" (15:13), but on the other hand they know that laughter can also be used to hide, rather than to heal, a sad heart (14:13). One person concludes that our deepest sorrows and joys cannot be shared (14:10). Another notes that a "heavy heart" cannot be lightened easily by another's songs (25:20). Others observe and comment upon the relationship between happiness and health: "A cheerful heart is a good medicine, but a downcast spirit dries up the bones" (17:22). Anxiety weighs us down (12:25), but "a tranquil mind gives life to the flesh" (14:30). Good news is like "cold water to a thirsty soul" (25:25). It can make our "bones" fat and juicy (an idiom for good health, 15:30), but "passion [jealousy or envy] makes the bones rot" (14:30). "Hope deferred" is said to make the heart "sick," but "a desire fulfilled" is "a tree of life" (13:12). A healthy "spirit" is said to help its owner endure sickness, while a "broken spirit" is more than most people can bear (18:14).

HYPOCRISY

There is no word in Hebrew to describe the human behavior which the English language calls hypocrisy, but several sayings indicate that the wise recognized its existence. The speaker in 27:5-6 says that wounds made by the "open rebuke" of a friend are preferable to profuse "kisses" from an enemy. The RSV rendering "hidden love" in v. 5 should be understood as insincere professions of love.

One of the "better sayings" favors persons "of humble standing" who work for themselves over those who pretend to be great but lack "bread" (12:9). Another saying apparently reflects the negative experiences of the speaker: many proclaim their loyalty, "but just try to find someone who really is!" (20:6 TEV).

The wise speak against those who make vows without intending to keep them (20:25), and "a man who boasts of a gift he does not give" is said to be like "clouds and wind without rain" (25:14). While human beings may not always be able to tell when someone else is being hypocritical, the LORD always knows who is sincere and who is not (see discussion of "Motives and Motivations" above, p. 75).

MISCELLANEOUS TOPICS

Old Age

If one assumes that long life is the result of wisdom and piety, as the wise often do, then it follows that gray hair "is a crown of glory; it is gained in a righteous life" (16:31). Gray hair is as much a "glory" for the elderly as strength is for the young (20:29). A saying mentioned under the topic of "family" may also apply here:

"Grandchildren are the crown of the aged, and the glory of sons is their fathers" (17:6).

Alcoholic Beverages

"Wine is a mocker, strong drink a brawler" observes one of the contributors to the Solomonic sayings, "and whoever is led astray by it is not wise" (20:1). Nothing more is said in the Solomonic sayings about the hazards of drinking, but the section of Proverbs called the "Sayings of the Wise" contains an extended poem on the topic (see the Commentary on 23:29-35).

Greed

Death and Destruction (personified as Sheol and Abaddon) "are never satisfied" and neither are the "eyes" of humankind, observes one of Hezekiah's men (27:20). But the wise consider greed both wicked (21:26) and unwise. Greed stirs up strife (28:25). Coveting, miserliness, and hoarding are counterproductive: a miserly person "hastens after wealth" without realizing that his or her actions will have negative results (28:22). A series of sayings in 11:24-26 speak to the same point: those who "withhold" what they should give will only come to want, while those who are generous will prosper.

THE FRUITS OF HUMAN BEHAVIOR

Proverbial statements by their very nature make only contextually limited claims to truth. Because circumstances differ, there can be no true unanimity of viewpoint expressed in a collection of pure proverbs. But the Solomonic collections contain a mixture of both proverbial sayings and theological assertions, both observations of reality and faith claims, both statements which comment on the way life is and those which speak of the way it should be. While some generalizations can be made about this body of literature as a whole, room must be left for the ever-present exception to the rule.

A close study of the Solomonic sayings indicates that those who formulated and handed these materials down to us believed that human actions have consistent and foreseeable consequences. Like the prophets, who speak constantly of the LORD's agency in the process of reward and punishment, some of the wise assert that the LORD oversees or disburses "rewards" (as in 19:17 or 25:22) and punishments (20:22) for appropriate or inappropriate behavior. More than one saying expects the LORD to provide some kind of sustenance for the faithful (10:3) and some kind of destruction for evildoers (10:29). One speaker even claims that "the LORD has made everything for its purpose, even the wicked for the day of trouble" (16:4).

The phrase "fear of the LORD" (meaning a reverent attitude towards God) is used eight times in the first section of Solomonic sayings. While this specific phrase is not found in the sayings copied by Hezekiah's men, there are two somewhat comparable sayings in the Hezekian collection which refer to "trust" rather than to "fear" of the LORD" (28:25; 29:25; cf. 16:20).

Four of the "fear of the LORD" sayings claim that this attitude of faithfulness towards God is directly related to attaining, prolonging, or enriching "life" (10:27; 14:27; 19:23; 22:4). In other places "fear of the LORD" is said to provide us and our children with "a refuge" (14:26; cf. 18:10), with instruction in wisdom (15:33), and with a way to avoid evil (16:6). The eighth usage is in the "better saying" which prefers "a little with the fear of the LORD" to "great treasure" accompanied by trouble (15:16). The speakers assume their listeners already know what it means to "fear the LORD" and are primarily interested in speaking about the results or the consequences which accompany this attitude which characterizes the faithful.

But many more of the Solomonic sayings use words such as "wages" or "rewards" without any reference to a divine intermediary or agent who is expected to dole out whatever it is that has been earned (e.g., 11:18). In fact the majority of cause-and-effect sayings in both Solomonic collections leave the LORD's name out. Instead, the speakers say that the wicked bring about their own downfall (14:32; 29:6) or that they are caught in the very traps they set for others (26:27; 28:10). There is what we might call "poetic justice" envisioned for those who wish harm upon their fellow human beings, rather than "punishment" imposed by some outside agency. One saying even comments that "some people ruin themselves by their own stupid actions and then blame the LORD" (19:3 TEV).

Quite a few proverbs use agricultural metaphors to refer to the "fruits" of human behavior (as in 11:30; 12:14; 13:2; 18:20, 21; 27:18). When the sages speak figuratively of "sowing" injustice and "reaping" calamity" (22:8), we receive the impression that they thought of actions and their consequences as a part of the natural order. Just as the seed and the fruit are alike in kind, so the speakers in these sentences expected to find a natural and observable congruence between an action and its "yield."

It is of course possible that those who avoid mentioning the LORD by name actually thought about cause and effect in purely secular terms. However, it might also be argued that the LORD does not need to be named among those who assume that their God is the source of the relationship they see between the "seed" and its "fruit." The reticence of many proverbs on the subject of the LORD's agency may be due to the observational nature of the proverbial endeavor. Instead of claiming that their wisdom comes directly from God, the makers of proverbs typically assert that "the hearing ear and the seeing eye" are gifts from the LORD (20:12). Thus, when they comment on what they can see and hear in the world around them, they believe they are using their God-given gifts in the way God intended. And while the LORD's agency may be *assumed* by the faithful, it is not an *observable* phenomenon.

When our ancestors in the faith collected and arranged these sayings, they included both proverbial statements about what is seen and statements of faith about the unseeable. In the final, canonical form of the tradition, the statements of faith have the effect of setting the stage upon which the observational proverbs perform. The faith claims provide the reader of the final product with a lens through which to read the whole. True "secularity" can be attributed only to sayings which are isolated and removed from the context in which our tradition has placed them.

THE SAYINGS
OF THE WISE

Proverbs 22:17–24:34

The first "Solomonic sayings" collection ends in 22:16 with a warning phrased according to the prevailing two-part statement format: those who oppress the poor to increase their own wealth and those who give to the rich "will only come to want." Then beginning with 22:17, the form of the literature changes back to the more loosely organized and didactically phrased style of poetry which characterized most of the first nine chapters of Proverbs. The commanding, coaxing style of speech (using second person forms of address) which prevails in 22:17–24:34 is very similar to that found in the Instructions in chs. 1–9. The address to "son" or "sons" is missing at first but occurs again in 23:15, 19, 26; 24:13, 21. Thematically speaking, there is little new to be found in this third section of the book of Proverbs. Most of the topics addressed in the "Sayings of the Wise" have already been considered either in the Instructions or in the Solomonic sayings. The phrase "sayings of the wise" occurs twice (in 22:17 and 24:23), which probably means that two originally separate collections have been combined in the present form of the text.

"Incline your ear," says the speaker to the listener at the beginning of the first collection, "and hear the words [sayings] of the wise," so that "your trust may be in the LORD. . ." (22:17-19; cf. 1:1-7). The phrase "sayings of the wise" may have ocurred originally as a title (as is still the case in 24:23), which was later incorporated into the body of the text.

THE "THIRTY" SAYINGS
(22:17–24:22)

The rhetorical question in 22:20 gives the first collection of the "Sayings of the Wise" its name. The word "thirty" is spelled unusually in the Hebrew, leading some translators to look for an alternate meaning for the word. Since a number of the sayings in this collection are strikingly similar to sayings found in the Egyptian Instruction of Amenemope, which also has thirty sections, the translation "thirty" seems to me to be relatively certain. However, the Hebrew text does not mark any such divisions, and there is no scholarly consensus on how best to divide the text into units. If we are to end up with exactly thirty sayings, we will have to make some slight adjustments in the order in which the verses are now found. (For a brief review of literature comparing Amenemope and Prov. 22:20–24:22, see Carl E. DeVries, "The Bearing of Current Egyptian Studies on the Old Testament.")

SAYINGS ONE TO FIVE (22:22-29)

"Do not rob the poor . . . or crush the afflicted at the gate" (22:22). The first saying in the "Words of the Wise" collection echoes the social justice concerns of Amos and Isaiah. Also, it uses the same words for "poor" (connoting weakness and helplessness) and "afflicted" (connoting those needy enough to be given gleanings) as the prophets frequently do when they preach against the oppressive legal practices which prevailed in Israel and Judah (e.g., Amos 2:7; 5:12; Isa. 10:2). The term "at the gate" refers to the practice of deciding legal disputes in the specially structured entryways to fortified cities. The hoped-for future king envisioned by Isaiah in Isa. 11:4 is expected to "judge" these helpless ones with "righteousness" (cf. Ps. 72), and the wise also expect the LORD to "plead" the poor's case (Prov. 22:23).

If the second saying of the collection (vv. 24-25) originally had any relationship to sayings one and three, it is not immediately apparent to modern interpreters. The idea it incorporates (that we learn from and become like those with whom we associate) is a fairly common concept in both the sentence proverbs and in the Instructions.

The sentiment of the third saying (vv. 26-27), which speaks against giving "pledges" (i.e., going into debt), is echoed in the Solomonic proverbs (e.g., 20:16) and in the Instructions (6:1-5). We would probably not see a logical connection between it and the references to the poor and the afflicted in 22:22-23 if it were not for the linking of similar ideas in Amos 2:6-8. The Amos passage reflects the custom of giving garments as surety for a debt. Those who were extremely poor could only give as collateral the cloak in which they slept, and the covenant made between Israel and the LORD demands that such pledges be returned "before the sun goes down; for that is his only covering, it is his mantle for his body; in what else shall he sleep? And if he cries to me [says the LORD] I will hear, for I am compassionate" (Exod. 22:26-27; cf. Deut. 24:12-13). Amos condemns those who callously disregard the rule, while the wisdom teacher simply counsels the pupil not to become one of those who have "nothing" with which to pay off their debts except their "bed." Taken together, the first and third sayings imply that even though the LORD will always be their advocate, those who are wise will try to avoid becoming one of the helplessly poor.

The fourth saying (Prov. 22:28) echoes a commandment found both in the Egyptian Instruction of Amenemope and in the legal codes of Israel (Deut. 19:14). The removal of a "landmark" or boundary marker would inevitably lead to disputes over the ownership of the land. Such disputes could be settled in court (in the gate?) or (quite often) through violence. Earlier in the Solomonic sayings we were told that the LORD guarded the "widow's boundaries" (Prov. 15:25), and again in the next chapter (in the tenth saying, 23:10-11) we will be told that "the fields of the fatherless" have an invincible protector. Since widows and orphans were nearly powerless in the society of ancient Israel, having very limited financial resources and no one to represent them in legal disputes, they are commonly said to be under the special protection of the LORD (e.g., Exod. 22:22; Deut. 10:18). Thus, in actuality this fourth saying is related to the first and third. Three of the first four "Thirty Sayings" therefore pertain to social justice.

The fifth saying (Prov. 22:29) is an enigma. Traditional renderings are based mostly on guesswork.

SAYINGS SIX TO EIGHT (23:1-8)

The phrase "do not desire his delicacies" occurs in both v. 3 and v. 6, leading some interpreters to suggest that v. 3 really belongs in the eighth saying (vv. 6-8). If v. 3 is moved, leaving only vv. 1-2 to make up the whole thought of the sixth unit, then the sixth saying would seem to be concerned with nothing more than table manners (i.e., do not be greedy when you eat at a ruler's table). However, if the present arrangement of the text is preserved, then the point of the sixth saying (vv. 1-3) is radically changed. If all three verses are included, the whole unit becomes a warning not to envy the ruler his delicacies, because they are "deceptive food."

I would argue that sayings six (vv. 1-3), seven (vv. 4-5), and eight (vv. 6-8) are all related in thought. They all advocate an attitude towards material possessions which is very similar to that found in the book of Ecclesiastes. The seventh saying phrases it most concisely: "Do not toil to acquire wealth; be wise enough to desist. When your eyes light upon it, it is gone; for suddenly it takes to itself wings, flying like an eagle toward heaven" (vv. 4-5). For the same reason one need not desire the ruler's delicacies (v. 3) because they have no permanent worth.

The point of the eighth saying is similar, though phrased in figurative language. The premise seems to be that those who are "stingy" (who tend to hoard their wealth) have an unhealthy attitude towards their possessions. Thus, sharing a meal (or indeed any form of communion) with such a person will do you no good. "You will vomit up the morsels which you have eaten, and waste your pleasant words" (v. 8).

SAYINGS NINE TO ELEVEN (23:9-14)

The subjects of vv. 9 and 12 are very similar. In order to come out with "thirty sayings," I suggest that vv. 9 and 12 be combined and designated the ninth unit in this section. Taken together they become an antithetical couplet, advising the listener both to avoid speaking within earshot of a fool and to apply his or her own "ear" to "words of knowledge."

The injunctions in vv. 10-11 against removing ancient landmarks and claiming the property of the fatherless (discussed above in connection with the fourth saying) would then be the tenth saying.

The eleventh utterance of the wise apparently comes from the same school of thought as the Solomonic sayings in 13:24 and 22:15. This advice in 23:13-14 has sometimes been taken literally and prescriptively and has had terribly destructive results. It ought to be understood as merely one culturally conditioned opinion among the many expressed by the various contributors to Proverbs.

SAYINGS TWELVE AND THIRTEEN (23:15-18)

The division of vv. 15-18 into two units of equal length is somewhat arbitrary. They could conceivably be two parts of the same saying. In the twelfth saying (vv. 15-16) the listener is once again called "my son," and the speaker assures this "son" that their interests are closely intertwined.

The thirteenth saying of the wise (vv. 17-18) has been the source of much speculative discussion. In the RSV vv. 17-18 seem to say that continuing "in the fear of the LORD all the day" will ensure that one's "hope will not be cut off" in the "future." The same phrasing is found in the second half of the twenty-sixth saying (24:14). Some interpreters think this statement reflects the speaker's hope for (or expectation of) a "beatific afterlife" for the faithful worshippers of the LORD. Others argue that the saying refers simply to hopes for the future in this life (with the idea that where there is life there is hope).

The traditional Israelite's expectation that both the righteous and the wicked will be "requited on earth" is expressed in a number of sayings in Proverbs (e.g., 11:31). But this thirteenth utterance speaks to the disappointment the faithful feel when they observe that "sinners" often seem to get away with their sins. This is also the subject of the twenty-ninth saying (24:19-20) and of Ps. 73, which may be closely related to Prov. 23:17-18. The psalmist complains that the wicked seem "always at ease, they increase in riches" (Ps. 73:12), while innocent and faithful worshippers of the LORD continue to suffer. This disparity between observed reality and the psalmist's expectations created a theological dilemma (Ps. 73:16), which the psalmist tells us was not resolved "until I went into the sanctuary of God; then I perceived their end" (v. 17). The word which the RSV translates "end" in Ps. 73:17 is the same word in Hebrew that is translated "future" in Prov. 23:18. The twenty-ninth saying states the converse as well: "the evil man has no future" (24:20). Whether one thinks the speaker's hope lies in this life or in another, the meaning of the opening lines of the thirteenth saying remain the same. "Let not your heart envy sinners, but continue in the fear of the LORD all the day" (23:17) is a word from the wise to the wise of both ancient and modern times.

SAYINGS FOURTEEN TO SEVENTEEN (23:19-28)

The four sayings in this section could easily be exchanged with one of the Instructions in chs. 1–9. Like most of the Instructions, the section begins with a call (which occurs first in 23:19 and is repeated in v. 26) for the "son" to pay attention. The fourteenth "saying" (vv. 19-21) sees a relationship between overindulgences and poverty, as did several of the Solomonic sentences (e.g., 20:13; 21:17). The drunkard, the glutton, and the chronically drowsy will all be clothed in rags, warns the sage.

The fifteenth (23:22-23) and sixteenth (vv. 24-25) sayings emphasize the stake both the father and the mother have in the child's proper upbringing. It sounds as though Wisdom personified might be speaking here, as she did in the Instructions. Ironically, the word translated "buy" in 23:23 is the same one which was translated "created" in 8:22.

The seventeenth statement (23:26-28) returns to a topic which was very popular in the Instructions. The word which RSV translates "adventuress" in v. 27 is the Hebrew *nokriyah* ("outsider, foreigner"). As explained in the commentary on earlier passages, "outsider" could refer to one who was outside the marriage covenant or outside the covenant community. Here in v. 27, *nokriyah* is parallel to *zonah* ("harlot"). Both are said to be traps (a "narrow well" and a "deep pit") which increase "the faithless among men." Once again the translations have failed to communicate the religious or cultic overtones which almost always accompany these terms in the OT. We are too easily tempted to draw analogies with modern practices of prostitution and to forget the way in which contributors to the OT used these terms in a figurative sense to describe Israel's faithlessness towards the LORD.

SAYING EIGHTEEN (23:29-35)

In seven short verses a sage with a keen sense of irony paints a vivid word picture of alcoholic addiction, complete with delirium tremens (vv. 33-34). The plight of the individual caught up in compulsive drinking does not seem to have changed much between the speaker's time and our own.

THE SAYINGS IN 24:1-22

With the exception of sayings twenty-two (v. 7) and twenty-five (v. 12), most of the remaining "Thirty Sayings" contain two verses, and each verse consists of two relatively balanced parts. There is a great deal of overlap between the topics addressed here and those covered in other sections of the book of Proverbs.

SAYINGS NINETEEN TO TWENTY-TWO (24:1-7)

Saying nineteen (vv. 1-2) echoes the opinion of violence given in 1:15-17 and reiterates the advice of 23:17 (not to envy evildoers). Saying twenty (24:3-4) uses the same imagery as 15:6. The structure which wisdom builds should be understood figuratively in both sayings. Neither the "house" of the wise nor the "riches" with which they fill it are meant to be understood as tangible (physical) possessions.

The twenty-first saying (vv. 5-6) restates the essence of 21:22 (the wise can vanquish the strong) and quotes the second lines of 20:18 and 11:14 with only slight alterations in wording. Again it is clear that the ability to seek out and make use of others' opinions is considered a hallmark of wisdom.

Saying twenty-two (24:7) consists of a single verse with two parallel phrases which makes an impersonal observation very much in the style of the Solomonic sayings. It is clear that the speaker's claim (that the fool does not open his mouth in the gate) has a limited range of application.

SAYINGS TWENTY-THREE TO TWENTY-SIX (24:8-14)

Each of the two verses I have included in the twenty-third saying (vv. 8-9) expresses a complete thought. Each could stand on its own, if necessary, but the theme upon which they both comment is the same: evildoers need to be named as such, and their sin needs to be branded as folly.

Most commentaries combine vv. 10-12 into a single saying, but it seems to me that v. 12 really ought to stand alone. Thus I have designated vv. 10-11 as the twenty-fourth saying. As a complete thought it condemns those who "faint in the day of adversity" and urges them to do something useful instead: "Rescue those who are being taken away to death; hold back those who are stumbling to the slaughter" (v. 11).

Verse 12 (the twenty-fifth saying) is longer than most other verses in the book of Proverbs. It actually consists of four relatively equal phrases (as do the majority of the two-verse sayings in ch. 24). In order to make sense of the verse, readers need to decide what is meant by the "this" which the speakers in the first phrase claim not to know. Those who read v. 12 as the conclusion to the saying in vv. 10-11 think that the speakers are claiming that they did not know what it was they should do on "the day of adversity." But if v. 12 is a complete saying, as I have proposed (i.e., if it is not logically connected to the verses which come before or after it), then the word "this" in the first phrase takes on a much wider meaning. In effect, I believe that the sage says that you cannot excuse yourself from responsibility in any matter by pretending you "didn't know," if in fact you did. There is, claims the speaker, One who "weighs the heart." Like the proverbs in 16:2, 9; 17:3; 20:27, the twenty-fifth saying of the wise is based on the assumption that the LORD can discern our motives and will "requite" us on this basis.

Saying twenty-six (24:13-14) compares the effect honey has on the tongue with the effect wisdom has on the whole person (RSV "soul"). Again, as in 23:18, we find a highly ambiguous saying about "the future." Here the claim is made that wisdom (rather than the fear of the LORD as 23:18 said) will keep one's "hope" from being "cut off." See the discussion on the thirteenth saying (23:17-18).

SAYINGS TWENTY-SEVEN TO THIRTY (24:15-22)

Sayings twenty-seven through thirty have a similar structure. Each begins with a piece of advice (in the form of a command) in the first verse and ends with a reason why the advice should be followed in

113

the second verse. We may find it easier to agree with the advice than with the extremely pragmatic rationales that are given.

Number twenty-seven (24:15-16) advises the listener not to do "violence" to "the dwelling of the righteous," because it would simply be a waste of time: the righteous person "falls seven times, and rises again" (v. 16).

Saying twenty-eight (vv. 17-18) begins with what sounds at first like an altruistic bit of advice: do not gloat over the downfall of your enemy. But the reason given is disconcerting: the LORD might see your reaction and be displeased by it. Thus the saying as a whole is clearly self-serving. Do not gloat, because gloating might reverse your enemy's misfortune (cf. 25:21-22).

The twenty-ninth "word" returns to the subject of the apparently unpunished sinner. For the third time in this collection of thirty sayings the "future" is mentioned, with a phraseology that *may* hint at the possibility that the speaker envisions some sort of reward or punishment taking place after an individual's death. However, it is clear that Job 21:17 does not understand the claim that "the lamp of the wicked will be put out" as a reference to an afterlife. When his friends tell him that this is the case (e.g., Job 18:5ff.; 20:5ff.), Job argues that the statement is patently untrue in his (and in others') experience. The wicked live, reach old age, and produce flocks of happy progeny, says Job (Job 21:7-12). "They spend their days in prosperity, and in peace they go down to Sheol" (Job 21:13) just as all other human beings do (cf. vv. 31-33). Thus, both Job and his friends seem to interpret the proverbial statement about the "lamp of the wicked" as a claim pertaining to one's future in this life, not to some other future. In Ecclesiastes, however, we will see that the theological question of retribution is raised anew with a suggestion of a new solution.

The collection of "Thirty Sayings," which began with references to the LORD, ends with a warning (Prov. 24:21-22) to fear and obey both the LORD and the king. The rationale given in this thirtieth saying is as self-serving as the ones which precede it. Since both the LORD and the king are capable of bringing down ruin upon their enemies, the wise will "not disobey either of them."

THE SECOND COLLECTION
(24:23-34)

The second collection of the "Sayings of the Wise" is much shorter than the first, containing either four or five sayings (depending on how the logical groupings are made). It begins with a simple announcement in the first half of 24:23 ("These also are the words of the wise"). The first saying begins with the second half of v. 23, which states the thesis upon which the following verses will comment: "Partiality in judging is not good." The following two verses simply elaborate on this thesis which is echoed in several different Solomonic sayings (17:15, 26; 18:5). The assumption which undergirds 24:23b-25 may be the one articulated in Isa. 26:10 (if the wicked are shown favor, they do not learn righteousness).

Prov. 24:26 may either be taken as further commentary on the subject of partiality (it is better to give an honest answer, even if it means rebuking the wicked), or it may be seen as a proverbial type of observation which is only casually related to its context.

The advice given in vv. 28-29 is worthy of notice. We are cautioned against giving false witness against our neighbors, even if we think they have done so to us. It is almost the "golden rule" in reverse: do not do unto others what they have done unto you.

The final "word" in this collection is five verses long (vv. 30-34). The sage speaks in a first person narrative form in vv. 30-32, describing a particular situation in life and thereby giving us the proper context in which to understand a saying which is found both here (in vv. 33-34) and in 6:10-11. The sage does not claim that all poverty originates in this way (see the discussion of the topic of poverty and prosperity in the Solomonic sayings sections above). The observation is simply made that this particular instance of poverty could be attributed to a lack of diligence.

SECTION FOUR
PROVERBS 30:1-31:31

THE WORDS OF AGUR
(30:1-33)

The second section of Solomonic sayings ends abruptly in 29:27 (with no discernible conclusion). The first half of 30:1 acts as a title or heading for the section which follows. In Hebrew the word *massa'* can be understood as a common noun meaning "burden" (sometimes used in prophetic texts in the sense of "oracle"), or it can be understood as a name. In Gen. 25:14 one of Ishmael's sons is said to be named Massa, so it is reasonable to assume that the term in Prov. 30:1 refers to a tribe whose ancestry was traced back to Ishmael. Since Ishmael was Abraham's firstborn son, the sages of Israel may have recognized that they had a "family" relationship (of sorts) with the people of Massa.

The RSV translates the second half of 30:1 as a statement addressed to two people (named Ithiel and Ucal). But as the text stands, the meaning of the words is a matter of guesswork. It is possible to read the original words as either common or proper nouns. In Hebrew there are no capital letter forms to help distinguish names from common nouns, and Hebrew names often make a meaningful statement. R. B. Y. Scott says the words are Aramaic for "There is no God, and I can" or "I am not God, and I can" (*Proverbs–Ecclesiastes,* 176). The NEB alters the text slightly in order to translate *ithiel* as "I am weary, O God," and *ucal* as "worn out," so that its version of 30:1b reads, "This is the great man's very word: I am weary, O God, I am weary and worn out."

THE BOUNDARIES OF KNOWLEDGE (30:2-6)

If only one person is speaking in vv. 2-6, then vv. 2-3 must have an ironic intonation. Agur's sarcasm seems to mock the pretensions

119

of those (perhaps Ithiel and Ucal) who claim that they have inside knowledge about "the Holy One" (literally, holy ones or holy things). The rhetorical questions in v. 4 are meant to be examples of truly unanswerable questions. Agur says, in effect, "If you are so smart, tell me the answers to these."

If vv. 2-4 make the point that true wisdom includes recognizing what you do not know, then the affirmation in v. 5 that "every word of God proves true" is being used to argue that the wise should not claim more knowledge for themselves than has really been granted to them by God. It is not wise to pretend you have answers to every conceivable question. "Do not add to [God's] words, lest he rebuke you, and you be found a liar" (v. 6).

NEITHER TOO MUCH NOR TOO LITTLE (30:7-9)

Agur says he asks only two things in order to be content: (1) to have the burden of dealing with lies taken away and (2) to have an income sufficient to his needs. The saying acknowledges the temptations which confront both those who have more and those who have less than they need. Overabundance tempts the rich to deny the LORD's sovereignty, while poverty tempts the poor to steal and thus profane God's name.

NUMERICAL AND OTHER SAYINGS (30:10-33)

Four sayings in this chapter conform to the same sequential numbering pattern we observed in 6:16-19. Each complete numerical saying in ch. 30 speaks of "three things" and "of four," and then goes on to name *four* things which fit in the category being considered. The sayings which follow this pattern are:

(1) Vv. 15b-16. Four things are said to be insatiable: the realm of death (cf. Isa. 5:14), a woman who wants but cannot have children (cf. 1 Sam. 1), the dry earth which seems infinitely capable of soaking up water, and fire which cannot exist without constantly being fed. The first half of Prov. 30:15 does not fit into the numerical pattern it precedes, leading scholars to conclude that something has dropped out of the text at this point. The meaning of the Hebrew word which the RSV translates "leech" is uncertain.

(2) Vv. 18-19. Four things (three from the natural world and

120

one from human experience) are said to be beyond the speaker's comprehension.

(3) Vv. 21-23. Four things are said to be too "heavy" for the earth to bear. Each "thing" mentioned in this saying seems to illustrate the elevation of a person from a disadvantaged to an advantaged position. The speaker apparently believes that such reversals in expectations ordinarily lead to intolerable arrogance on the part of the one who ends up on top.

(4) Vv. 29-31. The speaker names four kinds of strutting behavior. Three examples are drawn from the animal world, and the fourth is said to be that of "a king striding before his people." The RSV calls this a "stately" stride, but it is quite possible that the speaker is mocking the royal demeanor.

There are two more lists of four in this section of the text. One (in vv. 11-14) has no introductory formula at all but simply describes four kinds of unwise or sinful behavior without numbering them. The other (in vv. 24-28) lacks the first half of the numerical formula but names four types of small creatures who have a kind of wisdom which human beings could put to good use.

The sayings in vv. 10, 17, 20, 32-33 have no apparent logical or structural relationship to the rest of the chapter. However, some of them might be understood as commentary upon the actions described in vv. 11-14. Thus, v. 17 could speak of an appropriate type of punishment for the undutiful children described in v. 11, while v. 20 could be taken as an elaboration of v. 12. Verse 20 is of particular interest because of its vivid and yet euphemistically phrased description of an "adulteress." The technical term for adultery actually is used here (rather than one of the words for foreigner). Again, eating appears as a figure for sexual appetite, as was the case in the Instructions in chs. 1–9.

THE "WORDS" LEMUEL'S
MOTHER TAUGHT HIM
(31:1-31)

ABOUT RULING WISELY (31:1-9)

Again in 31:1 the word *massa'* may be understood as an ethnic designation (in which case the text reads, "The words of King Lemuel of Massa . . .") or it may be understood to mean an "oracle" (which would make the heading say, "The words of King Lemuel, an oracle . . ."). In either case the text is clear in its assertion that these are Lemuel's mother's teachings.

The opening words, "What, my son? What, son of my womb?" (v. 2), sound very much like a mother scolding her child. The word used here for "son" is in Aramaic, a language which is closely related to Hebrew. By the end of the 6th cent. B.C.E. Aramaic was the dominant spoken language in Mesopotamia. It was commonly used in official communications and would thus be familiar to most people in the ruling hierarchies of both Israel and other nations in the Fertile Crescent.

We might imagine a queen mother addressing a very young king or soon-to-be king, but no actual historical information is available. In vv. 3-4 Lemuel's mother seems to be questioning her son's behavior with regard to women and alcoholic beverages. Kings cannot let themselves be lured away from the serious business of ruling, insists the queen mother. The text does not say that women "destroy kings" but that the young king must not give his "strength" either to women or to anything else which might distract him from his responsibilities. Wine and strong drink are specified as the most likely distractions (v. 4). Alcohol could make the king forget what he should be doing and "pervert the rights of all the afflicted" (v. 5). This is not to say that wine does not have an appropriate use. In the queen mother's opinion, wine can be used as a sedative or as a pain-killer. It may be acceptable, she says, for the desperately ill to resort to strong drink (v. 6) or for the poor to drink in order to "forget their poverty" (v. 7), but a king needs to stay sober in order to do his duty!

Lemuel's mother holds up a rather idealistic picture of kingship for her son to follow. Clearly, she expects him to take an active role in upholding the rights of the powerless in his realm (vv. 8-9). This would not have been unusual among both Israelite and non-Israelite peoples in the ancient Near East. (See the discussion under the topic of "Kingship" in the Solomonic sayings.) Unfortunately, the prophets, the historians, and the wise in Israel testify to the repeated failure of kings to live up to the envisioned ideal.

THE CONCLUDING ACROSTIC (31:10-31)

The last twenty-two verses in Proverbs are in the form of an acrostic poem in which each verse begins with a new letter of the Hebrew alphabet in the traditional order. Interpreters argue over whether this acrostic poem should be considered a part of Lemuel's mother's advice or whether it is an independent (and thereby presumably "Israelite") composition. Some people think that the many sayings which speak so strongly against "foreign women" in other parts of the book indicate an attitude on the part of the wise which would not allow them to conclude the book with the words of a foreign queen. Others apparently fear that attributing the concluding words to a foreign queen mother diminishes the "authority" or the impact the poem might have on the reader. Claudia V. Camp suggests that "a poem about the ideal Israelite housewife—the mainstay of society in the post-exilic period—has been placed in the concluding (and therefore conclusive) position in the book . . . , displacing the instruction of a foreign queen" (*Wisdom and the Feminine in the Book of Proverbs,* 252-253). However, we have seen that the opinions of the collectors of Proverbs were not homogenous. Those who preserved the words of the wise for our edification frequently saw fit to juxtapose contradictory observations and claims. It is equally clear that those who finalized our whole canon of Scripture saw fit to include both the book of Ezra with its strictures against foreigners and the book of Ruth with its illustration of the role a foreign woman plays in the lineage of David. The xenophobia of one part of the postexilic community was balanced by other powerful claims that "foreigners who join themselves to the LORD" are perfectly acceptable in the LORD's house, which "shall be called a house of prayer for all peoples" (Isa. 56:6-7). Thus, it is by no means certain that those who made this poem into the conclusion for the whole book of Proverbs intended to divorce it from its apparent relationship to the words of Lemuel's mother. I suggest simply that our ancestors in the community of faith believed that this poem (regardless of its origins) made a fitting end to the first half of their two-volume collection of wisdom. They saw it as an integral and perhaps even as an indispensable part of what the "wise" had to say to their contemporaries and to us. Whether or not the material originated with Lemuel's mother, it is now a part of the way our ancestors witness to us through the Scriptures. And what they say to us is that the ideals of a wisdom way of life are the essence of what it means to "fear the LORD."

In Praise of a Woman who "Fears the Lord"

As the text now stands the acrostic seems to be the continuation of the queen mother's advice to her royal offspring. The word *(hayil)* which the RSV translates "good" in Prov. 31:10 (cf. KJV "virtuous," NIV "of noble character," NEB "capable") is the same word that is translated "strength" in v. 3 and "excellently" in v. 29. When this word is used elsewhere in the OT, it is usually understood as a reference to power (meaning either physical strength, strength of character, or will power). The best way to determine how the word should be translated in v. 10 is to pay attention to what else is said about the woman who is praised in the subsequent lines of the poem.

Whoever it is who speaks in vv. 10-31 says that the woman pictured here will be hard to find, but she will be worth her weight in precious stones to the man who is clever enough to marry her. He will be able to rely on both her abilities and her goodwill (vv. 10-12). He will discover that a woman who "fears the LORD" (v. 30) is worth much more to him than one who has only the perishable qualities of charm and beauty.

According to the poem, the range of this ideal woman's abilities and the reservoirs of energy and endurance from which she draws are truly formidable. She is pictured as organizing, overseeing, and tending to all the needs of a large estate, which includes the buying, selling, and planting of fields (v. 16). She is not adverse to hard physical labor (v. 17). She produces (or at least helps to produce) both the raw materials (vv. 13-14) and the finished products (e.g., clothing, food, footwear) needed by the members of her household, which includes servants as well as children (vv. 15, 19, 21).

She is engaged in commerce, making "linen garments" to be sold on the open market (v. 24). Her merchandise is "profitable" (v. 18), and she plans ahead well enough that she can cope with sudden emergencies (v. 21). The phrase, "Her lamp does not go out at night," could mean that she works far into the night (as well as getting up while it is still dark, v. 15). But more probably this refers to her foresight in providing herself with enough oil to burn (as in the parable of the five wise virgins at the marriage feast in Matt. 25:1-12). And best of all, in addition to everything else she does, "She opens her hand to the poor, and reaches out her hands to the needy" (Prov. 31:20).

At this point in the praise of the "ideal wife," the modern reader is probably inclined to ask where the woman's husband is and what he is doing while she is engaged in all these admirable (but undoubtedly exhausting) activities. "Her husband is known in the gates," we are told in v. 23, where "he sits among the elders of the land." If the passage as a whole describes the "ideal wife," then the comment in v. 23 is probably intended to serve as an inducement to the prospective husband. The implication seems to be that the husband is freed by his wife's activities to participate in the legal and judicial activities that take place within the city gates. While he is not precisely a man of leisure, his activities are certainly pictured as being less strenuous than hers. We may also get the impression that he has gained his respected position in the community primarily through his wife's endeavors.

The poem concludes with (1) a description in v. 28 of the rewards such a woman might expect to receive: her children and her husband constantly praise her, (2) a comment in v. 30 on what qualities are most valuable in a woman (the fear of the LORD is more enduring than beauty or charm), and (3) a final piece of advice: a woman like the one described here should be given "the fruit of her hands" as well as praise for what she does (v. 31).

As Camp aptly says, "While her husband nominally controls 'the fruit of her hands,' he is directed in no uncertain terms to give it to her" (91).

Some readers have suggested that this "wife" is nothing more than a figment of some man's imagination (a "dream woman" who frees him from all his responsibilities). She certainly could not be seen as a "typical" wife or as a model for all Israelite women to emulate, since the woman described in the poem clearly is thought of as a member of the affluent, landowning, or even ruling classes. She is not an ordinary woman but rather an extraordinary one. She is also said to speak with wisdom, and "the teaching of *hesed* ('faithfulness'; RSV 'kindness') is on her tongue" (v. 26), which would be in accord with the picture vv. 1-9 give us of Lemuel's mother. If this were Lemuel's mother picturing the kind of woman she would like for her son to marry, we might discount some of the details as wishful thinking on her part. On the other hand, the mother may be picturing some of the roles she herself has had to play in life.

However, I think the force of logic is on the side of those who see personified Wisdom mirrored in this down-to-earth and yet idealized picture of a skillful, prudent, and diligent woman who effortlessly manages her household and family affairs. References to Wisdom personified as a woman are scattered throughout the framework of the canonical form of Proverbs. We have seen how Wisdom has been poetically portrayed as a human female engaged in a variety of human occupations. Wisdom can act like a prophetess (1:20ff.), a darling child (8:30), a counselor to kings (8:15), a lover (4:6-9; 8:17, 21), a wife (as in 31:10ff.), or a mother (8:32ff.). She is a woman who "builds her house," fills it with treasures, prepares meals, and invites visitors in to participate in the feast she provides (9:1; 14:1; 24:3-4). The word translated "her household" in 31:21, 27 is the same as that translated "her house" in other passages. Wisdom, like the strong woman, is "more precious than jewels" (3:15) and is also capable of providing security for those who trust in her.

Thus, the concluding acrostic does not seem at all "foreign" to the images of wisdom which play a central part in the Instructions and a minor part in the other collections. Wisdom, who is pictured in the first chapter of Proverbs as a prophet of her own power and in the eighth chapter as a part of God's creative plan, is appropriately portrayed in the concluding portions of the book as a tower of strength for those who will trust in her ability to give them what they need (31:11). As Thomas McCreesh says, Wisdom "is not some lofty, remote ideal for those initiated into her mysteries, but a practical, ever-present, faithful guide and lifelong companion for all who choose her way" ("Wisdom as Wife: Proverbs 31:10-31," 46).

The collection which begins with the assertion that "the fear of the LORD is the beginning of knowledge" (1:7) thus ends with a hymn of praise for one who manifests in her life both the ideals of wisdom and the "fear of the LORD" (31:30).

APPENDIX

THEOLOGY AND PIETY
IN PROVERBS

DIRECT REFERENCES TO GOD

The thirty-one chapters in Proverbs contain fewer than one hundred specific references to Divinity. While the four-letter name *YHWH* (which scholars vocalize as "Yahweh" and translate as "LORD") occurs eighty-seven times, the generic terms *Elohim* and *Eloah* (translated "God" in the RSV) are used on only six occasions (Prov. 2:5, 17; 3:4; 25:2; 30:5, 9). In addition to these specific uses of "God" and "LORD," there are several oblique references to divinity, such as "Holy One" in 9:10; 30:3 and "Maker" in 14:31; 17:5.

Such references to God as occur are not uniformly distributed within the book. For instance "LORD" occurs eleven times in ch. 16, nine times in chs. 3 and 15, but not at all in chs. 4, 7, 13, 26, or 27. References to the "fear of the LORD" (which account for eighteen of the occurrences of the divine name Yahweh) also show an irregular pattern of distribution. This term (referring to an attitude of respect and loyalty towards the LORD and the LORD's intentions) is mentioned six times in the first nine chapters, eight times in the twelve chapters that make up the first "Solomonic sayings" section, twice in the first of the "words of the wise" sections (i.e., in chs. 23–24), once in the sayings attributed to Lemuel's mother, and not at all in the sayings which Hezekiah's men copied.

This clearly uneven distribution of terms may be the result of an editorial process. It is often assumed that the final canonical form of Proverbs is the product of a "Yahwistic reinterpretation" of an older, secular body of literature. If so, then our ancestors in the faith may be said to have "reframed" the whole, so that the secular

131

is now subsumed beneath the ruling assumption that the LORD God is both the source and the goal of wisdom endeavors.

Whatever may have been the process by which the book came to assume its final form, it may be argued that it is this present, canonical shape of the book which has influenced and continues to influence our communities of faith.

THEOLOGY

Very few of the direct references to God in the book of Proverbs are "theological" in the strictest sense of the term. In other words, one ought not to look for any systematic or speculative discussions of the nature or the attributes of God. No single saying, taken alone, provides us with a complete description of the nature or the purposes of God. Nevertheless, we can find clues to some of the theological assumptions of the contributors—clues to what they thought God was like—within their statements. When we consider the book as a whole, we find that each shorter utterance contributes a "stroke of the brush" from which a theological picture emerges. If we look, for example, at statements such as those which specify what things find favor or disfavor "in the sight of God," we can see that 6:16-19 pictures the LORD as one who values humility and truth telling and hates discord and the shedding of innocent blood. Other sayings claim that the LORD cares about fair dealing in commerce (e.g., 11:1; 16:11) and finds justice and righteousness more acceptable than sacrifice.

The Acts of God

In most books of the OT a reader could expect to find theological clues in statements about the acts of God (how God has been seen to act in the life of the individual or in the life of the faith community). But in Proverbs no mention is made of the Exodus or of the settlement in the "Promised Land" or of any of the other so-called "salvation events" in the history of Israel. In fact, just about the only statements made about what the LORD *has* done (in the past) concern the creation of the world in which we all live, (e.g., 3:19-20: "The LORD by wisdom founded the earth; by understanding he established the heavens . . ."; 8:22-31).

By far the majority of explicit statements about God in the book

132

of Proverbs speak to the present and to the future, making a variety of claims about what the LORD *is doing* and *can be expected to do* in the world. Such claims need not be seen as mutually exclusive. The LORD's creative activity is understood to continue into the present and to encompass both good and evil (16:4), both the oppressor and the oppressed (16:4; 29:13). The LORD is said to know and to evaluate human motives and intentions. Human hearts "lie open before the LORD" (15:11); the LORD "weighs the spirit" (16:2), "tries hearts" (17:3), and searches the "innermost parts" (20:27) of the individual. The LORD is expected to guard, protect, and smooth obstacles from the paths of those who are judged to be "good" or "upright" or "righteous" or "humble," and to punish or thwart the "wicked," the "deceitful," the "perverse," and the "arrogant." At the same time, it is assumed that the LORD disciplines or reproves those whom he loves (3:12). Of course the definition one gives here to the words must be a key factor in drawing theological impressions from such claims. If, however, we assume that the content of the wisdom *torah* (which is so frequently commended to the listeners in the "Instructions") was relatively congruent with the *torah* of Moses, then the specific behavioral content of righteousness and wickedness would have been quite clear in the minds of the teachers and their audiences.

Accountability

In some cases it is clear that the speakers in Proverbs expect the LORD to dole out material rewards and punishments during the normal lifetime of the recipient: "Honor the LORD with your substance and with the first fruits of all your produce; then your barns will be filled with plenty, and your vats will be bursting with wine" (3:9-10) or "The reward for humility and fear of the LORD is riches and honor and life" (22:4). Some interpreters think sayings such as 11:7 ("When the wicked dies, his hope perishes . . .") hint that the speaker may have expected some recompense for the righteous to reach beyond the grave. (See the discussion on "Afterlife," pp. 79-80 and 203-6).

However, the overwhelming majority of statements concerning the consequences that will result from various forms of human behavior do not mention God by name. Virtually hundreds of cause-and-effect claims are made without an explicit reference to divine agency or to divine intervention in the process. Such statements are inherently ambiguous. Taken in isolation (out of context), statements such as "Misfortune pursues sinners, but prosperity rewards the righteous" (13:21) or "Such are the ways of all who get gain by violence; it takes away the life of its possessors" (1:19) might be understood in a rather mechanistic way. The assumptions which the readers or the listeners bring with them to the text determine whether such statements are understood in a religious or secular way.

Of course those who did not refer directly to God in Proverbs might still have had God in mind. The "wise ones" of Israel may simply have assumed that their audiences would "read God in" to their sayings wherever it seemed appropriate to do so. In either case it is clear that the contributors to the book of Proverbs believed (1) that human beings have both the freedom and the ability to make choices, and (2) that all choices have consequences. The wise ones in Israel were convinced that human beings "must answer for and live with the consequences of" their choices (Walter Brueggemann, *In Man We Trust*, 82). When we look closely at Ecclesiastes, we will also find that Qohelet does not take exception to this idea of accountability. He simply questions traditional notions about the time and the manner in which such accountability will take place. In contrast to the majority opinion in Proverbs, Qohelet will argue that the consequences of our actions cannot always be seen "under the sun."

PIETY

At some point in the history of Judaism, people of genuine piety began to avoid saying the name represented by the consonants *YHWH*. When vowels were added to the Hebrew text (sometime between the 7th and 10th cents. C.E.), the vowels for the Hebrew word *adonai* (meaning "my lord" or "my master") were added to the consonants *YHWH* to help remind readers not to say the divine name out loud. From the earliest rabbinic traditions up to modern times, such circumlocutions as "The Name" or "The Holy One" have been substituted for *YHWH* in prayers. Even today many people of faith avoid saying or spelling out the name of God. Thus, the piety or secularity of a statement such as "The upright will inhabit the land" (2:21) or "the wicked will be cut off from the land" (2:22) cannot be judged solely on the presence or the absence of a specific reference to God.

I would argue that a speaker or a writer's choice of language (e.g., the use of traditionally religious terms such as "upright" and "wicked") and the overall context in which a statement occurs give us more reliable clues to the piety of the speakers in Proverbs than does the frequency of specific references to God. The "Beatitudes" in Matt. 5:3-12 might be considered roughly parallel in terms of language. Although statements such as "Blessed are the meek, for they shall inherit the earth," do not specifically mention God's agency, the terms which are used and the context in which they are imbedded combine to produce a religious rather than a mechanistic impression. If the wise ones of Israel were steeped in the traditions of their faith, they would undoubtedly associate such phrases as "loyalty and faithfulness" (from the Hebrew words *hesed* and *emet*) with the often repeated traditional affirmations that (a) the LORD possesses these qualities in abundance (e.g., Exod. 34:6; Ps. 25:10; 86:15; 108:4; 117:2) and (b) the LORD values these qualities in people (e.g., Hos. 4:1). Anyone who remembers that the LORD is "abounding in *hesed* and *emet*" and that the LORD condemns the people of Israel in Hosea's time because there is "no *hesed* or *emet* in the land" will probably hear religious overtones when these same words occur together in Prov. 3:3; 14:22; 16:6; 20:28.

Like beauty, piety and secularity are "in the eye of the beholder." Whatever origins any individual saying may have had, it is the collected body of sayings, taken as a whole, which has been reframed and handed down to us as a part of our Scriptures. The editorial process is also a part of our ancestors' witness to God's self-revelation in their lives. Even in its final form, however, the book of Proverbs does not now stand alone. The conclusion to the book of Proverbs brings us to the end of one set of answers to the question of what it is that is good for humans to do with their brief lives on earth. But the words of the wise do not end with the end of Proverbs. The book of Ecclesiastes has something more of great significance to contribute to the on-going discussion.

A Commentary on the Book of

Ecclesiastes

CONTENTS

INTRODUCTION

A ROSE BY ANY OTHER NAME . . . ?

"What's in a name?" asks the heroine of Shakespeare's *Romeo and Juliet*, "that which we call a rose, By any other name would smell as sweet" (act ii, scene 2, lines 42-43). Names do, however, have a way of shaping how we feel about the objects they designate. Roses would not be such popular gifts between sweethearts if we commonly called them stinkweeds or bloodsuckers! And the name given to a book has a very real power to shape our expectations of its purpose or its subject matter. We expect the title of a book to give us some clue to the type of material we are going to read. Thus, readers who recognize a similarity between the name Ecclesiastes and other English words meaning "of or relating to the Church" often expect to find some connections between the Church as they know it and the subject matter of the book. In the RSV these expectations are further heightened when the contents of the book are described in the first verse as the words of the "Preacher." Both of these terms are attempts to translate the Hebrew word *qohelet* into English. *Qohelet* (pronounced ko-*hell*-it) is a verbal noun meaning "one who assembles" or "one who calls (people) together." In Eccl. 7:27; 12:8 *qohelet* is used like a common noun, with a definite article, as if it were a title or a job description ("says *the qohelet*"). But elsewhere in the book the word is used without the article, like a person's name or nickname ("says *Qohelet*," in 1:1, 2, 12; 12:9-10).

When the Hebrew Scriptures were translated into Greek in the pre-Christian era, the word *qohelet* was translated into the Greek word *ekklesiastes*. In common usage *ekklesia* meant simply an assembly of people, and *ekklesiastes* referred to someone who called an assembly together. But the authors of the NT used the word *ekklesia* in a more specialized sense to mean "church," as in the phrase "on this rock I will build my *ekklesia*" (Matt. 16:18). Thus, several centuries after the first Greek translation of this book the word *ekklesiastes* acquired the sense of "a church leader."

In Hebrew, *qohelet* could refer to the activity of gathering together either an audience or a collection of sayings. Later tradition seems to have remembered Qohelet as one who "taught the people knowledge, weighing and studying and arranging proverbs with great care" (Eccl. 12:9). However, in modern English usage, "preacher" has acquired a rather specialized sense which does not really communicate the meaning of assembler or convener (of things or people). Therefore, in the following Commentary the name Qohelet will be used to refer to the primary speaker within the book, and the word Ecclesiastes will be used to refer to the book itself, that is, to the form in which the speaker's words have been handed down to us.

PIETY OR HERESY?

What will you find within the pages of this book called Ecclesiastes? Will you encounter the confessions of a true believer or the blasphemies of a heretic? Will your reading introduce you to a person steeped in cynicism or one who courageously faces and accepts the world as it is? For almost two thousand years faithful and well-informed interpreters have disagreed radically over the nature and purpose of these relatively short twelve chapters of Scripture.

Depending upon whom you read, you might conclude that Ecclesiastes is either "the quintessence of skepticism" or that it is "the quintessence of piety." Interpretive opinions range from the conviction that Qohelet's views run counter to the dominant teachings of the rest of Scripture to the assertion that they faithfully reflect the heart of the traditions and values of Israel.

How is it possible for one small book to generate such opposite and contradictory theories about its meaning? One important reason is the ambiguity of the thematic word *hebel*, which the RSV translates as "vanity." *Hebel* occurs thirty-eight times in Ecclesiastes, compared to only thirty-five other uses in all of the rest of the OT. Any word repeated so often in such a short space must leave a lasting impression on its hearers. But what does *hebel* mean?

EVERYTHING IS A PUFF OF AIR

In its simplest and most basic sense, *hebel* means "a puff of air," "a breath," or "a vapor." This sense of *hebel* can be seen in the RSV in Isa. 57:13: "The wind will carry them off, a *breath (hebel)* will take them away." R. B. Y. Scott's translation of Ecclesiastes in the Anchor Bible preserves this concrete, basic sense of *hebel* when he renders Eccl. 1:2 as "Breath of a breath! . . . The slightest breath! All is a breath!" (*Proverbs–Ecclesiastes*, 209). This translation enables English readers to see that the phrase "all is *hebel*" is actually a metaphor. The thematic statement of the book is expressed as a figure of speech. Like all other metaphors, it invites its hearers to look for the qualities that two essentially unlike things have in common. Both the speaker and the hearer of a metaphor know that the two entities which are compared are alike in some ways and unlike in other ways. Thus, when the poet Carl Sandburg tells us that "the fog comes on little cat feet," we can appreciate the poet's insight into the quality of movement shared by fogs and cats without expecting the fog to purr or to leave paw prints. Similarly, when we find that in Ecclesiastes everything "under the sun" is compared to a puff of air, we ought to consider what points of similarity there might be between these two essentially unlike entities.

Metaphors are intentionally provocative figures of speech which can be understood in quite different ways. For instance in Luke 13:20-21; 1 Cor. 5:6-7 "leaven" is used as a metaphor for both good influence and bad. It is possible, then, that *hebel* (meaning a puff of air) might be understood in either a positive or a negative sense. If the translation preserves the metaphor (as Scott does), the reader is forced to decide in what sense the comparison should be taken. In my opinion it is unfortunate that many modern versions of Ecclesiastes have chosen to take the decision away from the reader. Most translators obscure the metaphorical nature of the original statement and replace the concrete, nonjudgmental phrase ("breath" or "a puff of air") with various abstract terms—all of which have decidedly negative connotations in English. Even if a case could be made for replacing a metaphor with an adjective or a descriptive phrase, there are legitimate grounds for challenging the negative connotations of the words which many modern translators use to translate *hebel* in Ecclesiastes.

THE SEMANTIC RANGE OF HEBEL

In every language words have potential ranges of meaning, depending on how they are used in specific situations. When an ancient Near Eastern language such as Hebrew is translated into a modern Western language such as English, very few words can be said to cover exactly the same areas of meaning in both languages. Thus, if we examine every use of the word *hebel* in the OT, we find that a variety of English words have been used to communicate the different meanings *hebel* seems to have expressed in different contexts. A number of Psalms use *hebel* to describe the brevity of human life and the transitory nature of human concerns compared to the eternity of God and the durability of God's concerns. The RSV translates this sense of *hebel* as "breath" in Ps. 39:5, 11; 62:9; 78:33; 94:11; 144:4, but as "nought" in Ps. 39:6 and as "vain" in Ps. 62:10. Job also uses *hebel* as a metaphor for the brevity of life; the RSV preserves this meaning of *hebel* in "my days are *a breath*" (Job 7:16). The plural of *hebel* is translated in the RSV as "idols" (Ps. 31:6; Jer. 8:19; 10:8; Jonah 2:8). Similarly, the RSV translates the singular forms used in the phrase "they went after *hebel* and became *hebel*" (which is usually understood to refer to idolatry) as "worthless(ness)" in Jer. 2:5 and as "false (idols)" in 2 Kgs. 17:15. Both the KJV and RSV use the words "vain" and "vanity" for less specific usages of *hebel*, as in Prov. 31:30 and in Ecclesiastes.

These traditional renderings were undoubtedly influenced by the precedent set by Jerome, whose translation of the Hebrew Scriptures into Latin functioned as the authorized OT text for the Roman Church from the 5th cent. C.E. into the modern era. In commenting on his translation, Jerome noted that several early Greek translators had understood *hebel* in the sense of "vapor." But Jerome himself chose to follow the LXX's interpretation. Thus, Jerome replaced the concrete Hebrew noun *hebel* with the abstract Latin noun *vanitas* and its corresponding adjective *vanus*. The Latin terms include within their semantic range the meanings of "unsubstantial" and "lacking in permanence" as well as "useless, futile, or illusory." However, the English words "vain" and "vanity" do not cover as wide a range of meaning as do their Latin predecessors. In modern English usage "vanity" has the basic sense of "lacking in value." That which is "vain" is useless, worthless, or futile. But this may not be the sense which was conveyed to the initial audience of the original statement "all is *hebel*."

DOES LACK OF PERMANENCE MEAN LACK OF VALUE?

When we look closely at the ways in which the word is used in other parts of the OT, it becomes clear that the essential quality to which *hebel* refers is lack of permanence rather than lack of worth or value. A breath, after all, is of considerable value to the one who breathes it. However, it is not something one can hang on to for long. It is airlike, fleeting, transitory, and elusive rather than meaningless. Of course, if one tries to depend too heavily upon something which is essentially fleeting, one may suffer negative consequences. Thus Isaiah warns his contemporaries against depending too heavily upon Egypt as an ally, "for Egypt's help is *hebel* ('fleeting') and empty" (Isa. 30:7). Similarly, one might say that to worship or to give ultimate value to anything which is transitory is the essence of idolatry. Thus idols are "airlike," transitory, and lacking in substance, and those who "go after" *hebel* ("transitory-ness") will certainly "become *hebel*" ("transitory"). This sense of "ephemeral" or "fleeting" would fit very well in the passages in Psalms and Job discussed above. And in Prov. 31:30 the statement "beauty is *hebel*, but a woman who fears the LORD is to be praised" may very well mean that beauty simply is a less *enduring* quality to look for in a woman than piety.

Only one verse (the last verse in the book of Proverbs) separates Prov. 31:30 from Ecclesiastes in Christian Bibles. But ironically, some modern English versions (such as the NIV and NAB), which recognize that *hebel* means "fleeting" in Prov. 31:30 ("beauty is fleeting"), translate the same word two verses later (in Eccl. 1:2) as "meaningless" and "vain." It seems to me that this tradition of interpretation ignores the fact that in Ecclesiastes itself the word *hebel* is frequently paired with the word *ruah*, meaning "wind" or "spirit." In 1:14; 2:11, 17, 26; 4:4, 16; 6:9 *hebel* and *ruah* are virtually equated, lending a great deal of support to the supposition that the quality to which *hebel* refers is that of being like a puff of air, a breath.

In several of these verses (1:14; 2:11, 17) the pairing of *hebel* and *ruah* is also linked with the motif "under the sun," reinforcing the similarity between these statements in Ecclesiastes and the similar theme in the Psalms, where God's enduring qualities are contrasted to the impermanence of God's creatures.

DECIDE FOR YOURSELF!

Ecclesiastes has been understood in radically different ways by different readers in part because the thematic metaphor "all is *hebel*" is fundamentally ambiguous. Those who have taken *hebel* to mean "worthlessness, meaninglessness, or futility" have tended to see the author of the book as a man lacking in faith and piety and to see the book itself as an anomaly in the canon of Holy Scripture. Those who have understood *hebel* to refer to lack of duration ("transitoriness") have tended to see Ecclesiastes in a relatively positive light, especially when "fleetingness" is understood to apply to everything "under the sun" in contrast to the permanence of God.

Since most nonspecialists today must rely upon translations for access to the biblical texts, I would advise readers of the text in English to suspend judgment temporarily on the meaning of the metaphor and to substitute the phrase "breathlike" (or something similar) for every occurrence of the word "vanity" in the RSV. In this way they may allow the text to speak more clearly for itself before they draw interpretive conclusions about its meaning.

LINKING QOHELET WITH SOLOMON

Although the synagogue and the church traditionally have identified Qohelet with Solomon, the *name* Solomon does not occur anywhere in the book. Those who posit Solomonic origins point to Eccl. 1:1, "The words of Qohelet, the son of David, king in Jerusalem," and to v. 12, "I Qohelet was king over Israel in Jerusalem," to support their theory. Solomon was of course known as the prototype of wisdom leadership in Israel. However, the possible identification of Qohelet with Solomon is clouded by the use in 1:12 of a Hebrew verb indicating completed action or past tense, implying that the speaker's reign was then over ("I *was* king"). The biblical text knows of no time when Solomon might have made such a claim. Other statements in the book are equally difficult to reconcile with what we know about Solomon from other sources. For instance 1:16 and 2:7 imply many other kings

146

preceded him on the throne in Jerusalem, and 8:2-9 or 10:16-19 sound more like the opinions of a subject than those of a king. However, the fact that tradition did link Solomon's name with the origins of both Proverbs and Ecclesiastes may be further evidence that the "wise" who handed the texts down to us thought the two bodies of material belonged together in some way.

Most scholars agree that the Hebrew in which the present form of the book is written represents a very late stage in the development of the language. The text contains loanwords from Persian and Aramaic, and it uses certain vocabulary and grammatical forms which only became common shortly before the beginning of the Christian era. Recently, some linguists have argued that the peculiarities of Qohelet's language are due to other factors than the lateness of composition (e.g., Daniel Fredericks, *Qoheleth's Language*; Bo Isaksson, *Studies in the Language of Qohelet*), but most scholars think that the present form of the book must come from the Second Temple period at the earliest (i.e., from *at least* four centuries *later* than Solomon). However, since the fragments of Ecclesiastes found among the Dead Sea Scrolls are written in a script that seems datable to ca. 150 B.C.E. (James Muilenburg, "A Qoheleth Scroll from Qumran"), it seems clear that the book must have been completed prior to the middle of the 2nd cent. B.C.E.

"CONSISTENCY" OF VIEWPOINT

Several passages in Ecclesiastes contain comments *about* Qohelet rather than statements *by* him. At the beginning (1:1-2) and at the end of the book (12:8-10), as well as once in the middle (7:27), someone other than Qohelet speaks in the third person *about* Qohelet and about what he was known to have said and done. But in many places, beginning with 1:12, Qohelet refers to himself in the first person (using "I"). While it is clear that Ecclesiastes is not simply a collection of loosely related or unrelated sayings (as is most of Prov. 10–22), there is almost no agreement among scholars who have tried to find a discernible, logical progression in Qohelet's thought. (For a survey of opinions concerning the structure of Ecclesiastes, see Addison G. Wright, "The Riddle of the Sphinx: The Structure of the Book of Qohelet").

A careful, thoughtful reading of the book raises the question of whether all of the statements made in the first person sections of the book are equally advocated by Qohelet. In one verse Qohelet apparently asserts that "God will judge the righteous and the wicked" (3:17), and only two verses later he says that the fate of human beings is the same as that of beasts: "as one dies, so dies the other" (v. 19). In 5:4 he recommends that one pay one's vows to avoid God's displeasure, but in 9:2 he asserts that "one fate comes to all, to the righteous and the wicked . . . to him who sacrifices and him who does not sacrifice. As is the good man, so is the sinner; and he who swears is [the same] as he who shuns an oath." On one hand, the speaker apparently confesses, "I know it will be well with those who fear God . . . but it will not be well with the wicked," but on the other hand he asserts, "There are righteous men to whom it happens according to the deeds of the wicked, and there are wicked men to whom it happens according to the deeds of the righteous" (8:12, 14). Critics such as George Barton have found it "inconceivable that a writer should say in the same chapter, that the wise man and the fool have the same fate (2:15, 16) and that there is no good but eating and drinking and enjoying one's self (2:24), and also say that God punishes the sinner and rewards the good (2:26)" (*Ecclesiastes,* 44). Thus Barton, and many other readers of the text, have felt "compelled" to conclude that those statements which *both* contain orthodox Jewish doctrine *and* contradict other statements in the book must be from the hand of one or more editors or glossators who added phrases and/or passages to the original statements of Qohelet in order to make the original conform to their own notions of faith and piety.

Other readers have tried to account in other ways for the apparent tensions within the book. If one assumes that the book is the result of (or is shaped in the form of) either a dialogue between a pupil and a teacher or a forum in which various individuals' opinions are aired, then variations in viewpoint are easily explained. There are, however, no indications in the text itself that this is the case. Some analysts have suggested that Qohelet's style is deliberately dialectical: sometimes he quotes the opinions of those with whom he disagrees in order to refute them, and sometimes he uses a "Yes, but" style of discussion which attempts to show the nonabsolute nature of many propositions commonly accepted as truths. (For a thorough survey of various approaches to the contradictions in Qohelet, see Michael V. Fox, *Qohelet and His Contradictions,* esp. 19-28).

I would like to suggest that most of the material in Ecclesiastes fits into the category of "journaling" (the process of keeping a reflective journal) better than it conforms to our modern notions of a treatise or a reasoned argument on a single subject. In many sections of the book, Qohelet speaks of his own inner deliberations. Although an audience is implied, it is seldom addressed directly. There is little of the urging, commanding style associated with the Instructions in Proverbs. Instead, Qohelet seems to allow the audience to "overhear" his reflective meditations.

However, I caution the reader not to expect every difficulty in understanding Qohelet to be resolved by any one theory. As John Barton quite correctly points out, "It is easy for us to assume . . . that we know what would constitute a coherent or consistent piece of writing in any literate culture, and to forget how far ideas like consistency . . . are dependent on convictions that vary from culture to culture" (*Reading the Old Testament*, 135-36). We ought not to expect Ecclesiastes to conform to our own literary conventions or to follow what *we* would call an orderly, logical plan of either journaling or argumentation.

QOHELET'S "IMPLIED" AUDIENCE

While we cannot locate a precise historical setting for Qohelet or his (implied) audience, clues in the text support some speculations about the worldview and the social location of those to whom Qohelet's remarks originally were addressed. Members of the audience seem to have had a certain degree of affluence: Qohelet assumes they are working to acquire possessions over and above basic subsistence-level needs (e.g., 4:4; 5:12). The frequently repeated advice to "eat, drink, and enjoy" the work God has given one to do indicates that the listeners have enough resources to lift them above the minimum level needed to sustain life. Furthermore, both Qohelet and his audience seem to have been concerned with "gathering and heaping" (2:26) the kinds of things which could be handed on to their heirs (2:18-21; 4:7-8; 5:13-17). Thus, it seems clear that Qohelet speaks as one of the affluent to others whose resources exceed their needs.

Qohelet's attitude towards poverty (and towards the oppression which he recognizes as one of its roots) is that of a sympathetic observer (e.g., 4:1; 5:8). Oppression is something he notices happening to others, but it does not appear to be an existential issue either for him or for the majority of his audience. Furthermore, he seems to have assumed that at least some members of the audience had regular access to the royal court (e.g., 8:2-4). Thus, most clues point towards a "middle-class" or "upper middle-class" audience for the bulk of this work.

Qohelet and his audience may have been well grounded in traditional beliefs, but there are indications that some new and as yet unresolved issues are "in the air." Qohelet compares some of the traditional affirmations of wisdom with his own experiences and finds that there is a "cognitive dissonance" between what he has been taught to believe is true and what he observes really happens in life. The wise may have said that their teachings were a "fountain of life, that one may avoid the snares of death" (Prov. 13:14), but in Qohelet's experience "the wise man dies just like the fool!" (Eccl. 2:16).

There are some indications that Qohelet and his audience may be considering new ways to reinterpret the old traditions. For instance the frequent use of the term "under the sun" in this book seems to indicate that either the audience or the speaker had begun to speculate about life after death as a way of resolving the dissonance between traditional retributive expectations and observed reality.

The phrase "under the sun" occurs twenty-nine times in the manuscripts used by the RSV, at least once in every chapter except ch. 7 which uses a similar sounding "those who see the sun" in 7:11. "Under the sky" (RSV "under heaven") occurs three times (in 1:13; 2:3; 3:1) and "on earth" has a similar meaning in 5:2; 8:14, 16; 11:2. Although references to any sort of afterlife are rare in the rest of the canon of Hebrew Scriptures, the frequency with which Qohelet uses these related phrases seems to indicate it is a subject of interest or importance to him (or to his audience). Qohelet seems to hint that a distinction can be made between what happens on earth, "under the sun," and what happens elsewhere. But he also asserts that human beings cannot know anything for certain about "what comes after" our lives on earth (cf. 3:21; 6:12; 7:14). This may indicate either that his audience has been speculating in ways which Qohelet hopes to discourage or that he is encouraging or provoking them to consider ideas which previously had not been included or developed in their traditions.

How Does It All Hang Together?

Without imposing our own canons of consistency on the book, it is possible to come to some agreement over the symmetry of the patterns of "catchwords" or repeated phrases in the book as it now stands. (See Wright, "The Riddle of the Sphinx"; and Roland E. Murphy, *Wisdom Literature*, 128-29). For instance the phrase which the RSV translates "vanity and a striving after wind" occurs seven times between Eccl. 1:14 and 6:9. (Two more uses of "striving after wind" occur in 1:17 and 4:6 without the word "vanity.") Then, although "vanity" continues to occur in every chapter except ch. 10, "striving after wind" disappears and is replaced in 6:12–11:6 with phrases that question or deny humanity's ability to know anything for certain "under the sun." In the final half of the book the phrases "who can/cannot find out" occur four times and "do not know"/"no knowledge" occur six times.

These linguistic patterns do not necessarily correspond to patterns of content or meaning. However, at the risk of appearing to add just one more straw to the haystack of opinion, I would like to suggest that the structure of Qohelet's argument is something like the structure of a mobile or a windchime (one of those decorative constructions in which various pieces are suspended on threads or wires and balanced in such a way that each part is able to move independently in a breeze, and yet each part depends on another for its equilibrium).

It seems to me that 6:12 could be considered the pivot from which two distinct parts of Ecclesiastes swing. Both sections depend upon the question, "Who *knows* what is *good* for humankind?" Chapters 1–6 concentrate on the question of "what is *good*," and chs. 7–12 explore the question of human *knowing*.

In chs. 1–6 two possible answers hang on the question "What is good?" Both hard work (or its resultant material benefits) and wisdom might be said to be good, but they each have limitations, which are spelled out for us in various ways. Neither emerges from Qohelet's examination as something which can be relied upon ultimately. In the second half of the book, the thought of the inadequacy of wisdom is pursued in the form of questioning "who knows?" and of spelling out the things "no one knows" for certain. The premise from which all of these elements are suspended is the assertion, "all is *hebel* . . . under the sun."

CHAPTER ONE

TITLE AND THEMATIC SUMMARY (1:1-2)

On the cover of a modern book we often find a brief description of its author and a short summary of its subject matter. These first two verses of Ecclesiastes may have served a similar function for an ancient audience. Any descendant in the Davidic line could have been called a "son of David." The description may have been based on Qohelet's own statement in Eccl. 1:12. The phrase which a later generation (or an editor) thought best identified the content of Qohelet's teaching is a superlative construction, meaning "the most breathlike of all breaths." The phrase is repeated in this complete form once more in 12:8 as a part of the editor's summing up of Qohelet's work. Thus, in the form of text handed down to us, the body of Qohelet's work begins and ends with this provocative metaphor: "all is *hebel*."

WHAT REMAINS WHEN THE WORK IS DONE? (1:3)

The discussion of what is worthwhile for humans to do during their brief lives under the sun begins with this provocative query: What do we "gain" (literally, "what remains" or "what is left over") from all our hard work on earth? If *hebel* means "breathlike," then the question of "gain" acquires the sense of "what is *permanently* gained?"

THE THEME OF THE FIRST HALF OF THE BOOK

All of chs. 1 through 6 can be grouped rather loosely under this larger topic of "What is good [or worthwhile] for humans to do during their brief lives on earth?" This is what Qohelet says he set

152

out to discover (in 2:3), and this is the question which closes the discussion in 6:12. Qohelet spends the better part of six chapters considering the types of "goods" people work hardest to attain. Some people work hardest to attain wisdom, some to attain power, some to accumulate possessions, and some in the hope that they will make a mark upon the future. Qohelet challenges his audience to think, first of all, about what they really gain from their work. Does there have to be something tangible "left over" from your labors in order to make them seem worthwhile? Using observations from nature, from general human experience, and from his own personal experiences, Qohelet will argue that none of the good things we work so hard to acquire are permanent or enduring. This is not to say that work or the things which are gained through work are without value. They are like a breath, which is precious to the one who breathes it. But also like a breath, they cannot be grasped and kept. The lesson the audience learns as they accompany Qohelet in his meditations is similar to that taught by the story of God's giving of manna to the people of Israel in the wilderness. God intends for us to use and enjoy the gifts that we are given, not to hoard them or to store them up for the future.

THE CYCLES OF NATURE (1:4-11)

The question Qohelet raises in 1:3 is not whether there is any *value* in what happens "under the sun" but whether there is any *permanence,* anything which can be grasped and kept ("gained"). In vv. 4-11 Qohelet uses the observable phenomena of nature and the human senses to point towards an answer to his question. The evidence which comes from the observation of natural processes indicates that nothing is left over from one cycle of nature to another. A generation of human beings comes and goes much as the sun rises and sets, or as the wind blows, or as streams flow. No sunshine is left over from day to day—the sun needs to do its work over and over. All the processes of creation on earth are transitory or fleeting *(hebel).* Only the earth itself, the stage upon which these processes take place, "remains for ever."

The RSV translation in v. 8 ("all things are full of weariness") is misleading. Hebrew *debarim* can mean both "words" and "things." Since the rest of the verse has to do with seeing and hearing, it would be better to translate this phrase as a parallel having to do with speaking. The sense of the whole seems to be that no one can say everything there is to be said, because words, like sights and sounds, are *hebel* or "breathlike." Speaking, seeing, and hearing are all things which have to be done over and over again. Our eyes and our ears cannot fill up with the sights we see or the sounds we hear, because sights and sounds cannot be grasped and kept any more than words which are uttered can be stored up or left over. Verses 9-11 claim that everything "under the sun" is recycled. Those things which seem new to us have merely been forgotten as previous generations passed away. Furthermore, Qohelet declares, future generations will not remember what happened in our time. Nothing *under the sun* (no process of nature and no product of human endeavor or ingenuity) is permanent.

Many readers will be disconcerted by this assertion that we gain nothing permanent from all our labor. Does Qohelet's argument take away human incentives for work (as some critics have said), or does it merely place our human ambitions in a realistic perspective with relation to the rest of the cosmos? Many of us hope we will leave a permanent mark on the world by our presence in it. Qohelet gently but firmly depresses our pretensions. Since this entire section of Ecclesiastes opens with a question about *human* achievements ("What do humans gain from all their toil?"), there is no reason to conclude that Qohelet is projecting limits to what *God* might do. Qohelet does not include God's activities in the category of what is done "under the sun."

SOLOMON HIMSELF WOULD SAY . . . (1:12-18)

The use of the completed-action form of the verb (suggesting "I used to be king") gave rise to an early Jewish legend that Solomon went by the name Qohelet after he had been dethroned by the "king of the demons." It seems much more likely that Qohelet is here playing a role in order to argue a point. He uses the form of a self-introduction to pose a type of riddle. In effect he is saying, "Given these clues (I was king over Israel in Jerusalem and known for my wisdom), guess who I am?" Then Qohelet uses the facts of Solomon's life (which would have been well known to his audience through their traditions) to argue that even one who had all the wisdom and wealth of Solomon would come to the same conclusions as Qohelet has: "all is breathlike."

According to v. 13, Qohelet first set out to explore "all that is done under heaven." Later he will tell us that this is something no human being can in fact discover (3:11; 8:17). But when he first applied his mind to this task, he thought it was possible. It is unclear whether the "unhappy business" he thinks God has given humans to do refers to the business of searching out everything under the heavens or whether he means that all human activity is unhappy or unproductive. The word for God which Qohelet uses here (and indeed all the way through his work) is *Elohim*. The personal name Yahweh (LORD) which occured so often in Proverbs is not used at all in the book of Ecclesiastes. The term "striving after wind" (which occurs for the first time in 1:14) might also be translated "feeding on wind" or "herding the wind," as the same Hebrew phrase is translated in Hos. 12:1: "Ephraim *herds the wind,* and pursues the east wind all day long." In any case the sense seems to be that there would be no profit or gain from such an endeavor. Here, Qohelet says that his search for everything that is done leads him to the conclusion that anything "done under the sun" will have the same ultimate "gain" as the activity of chasing or herding the wind. This phrase will occur again in Eccl. 2:11, 17, 26; 4:4, 16; 6:9, but it is not used at all in chs. 7–12.

Eccl. 1:15 resembles the two-part parallel sayings found in Prov. 10–22. The first half of the verse occurs again in Eccl. 7:13. It is difficult to say whether Qohelet used a traditional saying to further his argument (in which case it would equate "striving after the wind" with trying to straighten what is crooked or number what is not there) or whether this is a gloss—a comment by a later reader which has been incorporated into the present-day text (in which case it would seem to be a derogatory remark). In 1:16-17 Qohelet claims (either for himself or for Solomon) the highest degree of wisdom ever acquired by a ruler over Jerusalem. And yet this wisdom itself tells him that the effort one needs to expend in order "to know wisdom and to know madness and folly" cannot produce permanent results: "This also is but a striving after wind."

Another statement made in traditional proverbial form (v. 18) ends this part of the discussion with a surprising twist: it might even be argued that the search for wisdom is counterproductive. The more you know, the more you can see the insoluable problems which confront you. Verse 18 may reflect the same attitude towards knowledge as does the story in Gen. 3. When humankind first tasted the fruits of "the tree of the knowledge of good and evil" their immediate reactions were those of embarrasment and anxiety. In Eccl. 2:12-16 Qohelet will reflect further on both the advantages and the limitations of wisdom. In ch. 3 and throughout chs. 7–12, Qohelet will illustrate his conviction that wisdom has God-given boundaries.

CHAPTER TWO

THE "CONFESSIONS" OF A CONSPICUOUS CONSUMER (2:1-11)

The chapter changes, but not the topic of conversation. The speaker is still considering the question posed in 1:3 (Is there anything which can be grasped and kept from all the hard work we do under the sun?). Here in the second chapter Qohelet turns from pointing to natural phenomena (which everyone can see) as evidence for his argument to a more confessional mode. The first three verses serve as a framework for the "journaling" which follows. Qohelet tells us that he has experimented with various forms of human activity to see whether he could find out "what was good" for humans to do during their brief lives "under heaven" (2:3). The title of Harold Kushner's book about Ecclesiastes (*When All You've Ever Wanted Isn't Enough*) is an accurate summary of the contents of this chapter. Someone like Solomon, who could be said to have done almost anything he wanted to do and to have possessed everything his eyes and his heart desired, makes a convincing witness to the ultimate lack of satisfaction such things give to the one who has them. The conclusion Qohelet draws from his experimentation is this: hard work is useless if one does it only to acquire material possessions. The value hard work has is the pleasure one feels in doing it (v. 10), but no amount of work can produce material benefits that can be grasped and permanently gained "under the sun" (v. 11).

IS WISDOM WORTH WORKING FOR? (2:12-16)

In 2:12-16 Qohelet resumes the discussion which left off in 1:18. If Qohelet himself had once been inclined to take Prov. 13:14 and its parallels literally, his experiences in life have pushed him to reconsider his assumptions. The wisdom Qohelet has worked so hard to attain now allows him to see, on the one hand, that both the wise and the foolish person will inevitably die (Eccl. 2:14 and 16), and that neither will be remembered forever. Their eventual destinations are the same. On the other hand, asserts Qohelet, this does not mean that wisdom is totally without value to those who attain it. The wise and the foolish travel in different ways towards their mutual destination. The wise have eyes in their heads and walk in the light, while "the fool walks in darkness" (v. 14). Thus, the answer Qohelet gives to the question of whether wisdom is worth working for is, "Yes, but. . . ." Yes, it is better to be able to see where you are going but don't expect wisdom to save you from the fate common to all living things. This topic will be taken up again in 9:13-18.

THE ROAD TO DESPAIR (2:17-23)

Qohelet confesses in 2:17-21 that his experimentation led him initially to despair. He had placed great value on what he had been able to accomplish "under the sun." When he finally realized that he too would have to die and that everything he had worked so hard to acquire would have to be left behind him "to be enjoyed by [someone] who did not toil for it" (v. 21), he fell into a deep depression (v. 20).

Qohelet tells us what his experimentations and his wisdom helped him discover: human effort cannot create anything which may be relied upon to endure. His observations have led him to the conclusion that excessive work, "toil and strain," will produce little other than insomnia and pain (vv. 22-23). It may be true in some circumstances that "the hand of the diligent makes rich" (Prov. 10:4), but Qohelet concludes that even if you drive yourself to the point where your work becomes nothing more to you than "vexation" and pain, the results of your labors will still be *hebel*, as transitory as a breath.

THE GIFT OF ENJOYMENT (2:24-26)

Qohelet's despair is also *hebel*. It does not endure forever. Qohelet's disappointment turns to acceptance when he learns to appreciate

158

the ability God gives us to find enjoyment in our work. Qohelet concludes, using reason based on experience, that God intends for us to get sustenance and satisfaction from our labors and nothing more (Eccl. 2:24-25). Furthermore, Qohelet asserts that the ability to find value and joy in the work we do is a gift from God. Ironically, Qohelet suggests that it is not the righteous who have the most to show from their labors. Those who are frantically engaged in gathering and heaping up possessions are actually "sinners" (from Hebrew *hata'*, meaning they have "missed the mark"). The fruits of such frantic labor will be given to someone who pleases God (v. 26).

The chapter ends with the enigmatic phrase, "This also is *hebel* and a striving after wind," and again the antecedent of "this" is unclear. It may be taken to mean that however one acquires an abundance of possessions (either by one's own labors or as an unearned gift), these possessions are "a breath" which cannot be relied upon to endure.

CHAPTER THREE

EVERYTHING IS "BEAUTIFUL" (3:1-11)

Several themes in ch. 3 have been used in popular song lyrics. Thus, the poem in 3:1-8 may sound more familiar to North Americans than any other passage in Ecclesiastes. Unfortunately, the words used in the songs have quite a different meaning when they are taken out of context than they do when they are read as a part of Qohelet's argument. As v. 9 reminds us, Qohelet is still considering his initial question of what "gain" workers can expect from all their toil. Again the question concerns *permanent* gains.

The words translated "season" *(zeman)* in v. 1 and "time" *('et)* in vv. 1-8 have been understood in a variety of ways. Some interpreters think that *'et* refers to an "appointed time," that is, to a predestined period set aside for each of the purposes described. This understanding would bring the poem in line with the attitude expressed in Prov. 16:4 ("The LORD has made everything for its purpose, even the wicked for the day of trouble"). However, *'et* is used in many OT passages with the sense of "an appropriate time," and this is the meaning which best fits into Qohelet's discussion. The word which is translated "beautiful" (v. 11) in the RSV might be better rendered as "excellent" or "praiseworthy" in this context.

Qohelet asserts that there is an appropriate time for almost every human activity imaginable. However, he does not presume to say that he knows when these times are. Rather, he makes a somewhat startling claim. God has "put eternity" into human minds in such a way that we "cannot find out what God has done from the beginning to the end" (v. 11). God has implanted in us an awareness of our inability to know everything we want to know. And God has made everything beautiful (praiseworthy) in its (appropriate) time, but God has done so in such a way that we humans cannot find out for sure which *times* are appropriate for which

160

activities. In the song lyrics, the statement "everything is beautiful in its own *way*" makes quite a different kind of claim.

Since Hebrew has no grammatical neuter, the pronoun translated "its" (in *its* time) is actually masculine singular, raising the possibility that the sentence should be understood to mean that God makes everything beautiful in *God's* own time. In either case it remains clear that Qohelet is declaring that we humans do not have any way to determine for ourselves what God has in mind or what God sees to be appropriate behavior in any given time. The theme of the inability of human knowledge to comprehend the enormity of God's works will be taken up again in ch. 8.

Many of the contributors to Proverbs tended to make absolute judgments about the nature of good and evil. It would be easy to conclude from the bulk of proverbial wisdom that some forms of behavior are inherently evil and are never appropriate. But Qohelet makes a radically different claim. He says that circumstances determine whether a given action is good or bad. Even war and hate might be appropriate in certain contexts. Like the wise who listed totally opposite pieces of advice one after another in Prov. 26:4-5, Qohelet implies that a given action can be either right or wrong, depending on what else is going on when it is done.

ENJOY YOURSELF (3:12-22)

There is a thread of logic which ties Eccl. 3:1-11 to the remainder of the chapter. Given the premise that God has purposes which will always remain unknown to us, argues Qohelet, we can conclude that we ought not to expend too much energy or anxiety in trying to guarantee that our actions will have permanent results. Whatever God does will "endure" forever. We can neither add to nor take away from that which God has done (v. 14).

Qohelet is convinced that God intends for us to "take pleasure" in what we do during our brief lives on earth (vv. 12-13). This is not to say, however, that anything which gives pleasure would be approved of by God. Qohelet clearly draws some conditions around the nature of the "pleasure" God intends for us to have, by referring in vv. 16ff. to righteousness and wickedness. It is not Qohelet's opinion that "everything goes." Rather, Qohelet advises his audience to relax and enjoy their brief lives on earth (vv. 12-13), trusting that the God who has "appointed a time for every matter, and for every work," will also appoint a time to "judge the righteous and the wicked" (v. 17).

Qohelet tells us, on the one hand, that he believes in his heart that God will judge the righteous and the wicked. But on the other hand, he argues with those traditions in Israel which claim that human behavior is rewarded or punished "under the sun." As evidence against the proverbial claim that the righteous and the wicked are requited on earth (Prov. 11:31), Qohelet refers to his own observations: "I saw under the sun that in the place of justice, even there was wickedness, and in the place of righteousness, even there was wickedness" (Eccl. 3:16). In spite of the claims so consistently made by the proverbially wise, Qohelet argues that his own experiences in life indicate to him that human beings do not always receive their "just desserts" *under the sun.* But, in his meditations, he concludes that if God truly has "appointed a time for every matter" (v. 17), then it logically follows that God also has appointed a time for judging between the bad and the good.

There is a clear contrast between what Qohelet "says in his heart" and what he sees with the evidence of his God-given powers of observation. In his commentary on Eccl. 3:16-22, R. B. Y. Scott concludes that Qohelet stands over against "the orthodox answer . . . that God's judgment will eventually set things right" (*Proverbs–Ecclesiastes,* 223). I think, however, that this was not yet the "orthodox answer" in Qohelet's time. The orthodox answer (judging from the bulk of Proverbs, Deuteronomy, and the Deuteronomic histories) was that God's judgment would set things right "under the sun." But here Qohelet is suggesting that the discrepancies which can be observed when one compares orthodox expectations with human experiences can be explained only if the "appropriate time" for judgment is not limited to our lives "under the sun."

However, Qohelet does not want his audience to come to this conclusion too easily. In vv. 19-22 he reminds us that the evidence of our senses indicates to us that human beings and animals have a similar fate: "as one dies, so dies the other" (v. 19). The word "advantage" in v. 19 is from the same root as "profit" and also means "what is left over." All living things "are from the dust, and all turn to dust again" (v. 20). There is nothing at all to indicate whether humans have something more left over or whether "the spirit of man goes upward and the spirit of the beast goes down to the earth" (v. 21).

162

It is possible, however, as Qohelet suggests in v. 18, that this lack of concrete evidence may be God's way of testing our faith. The understanding of life and death presented here is well within the mainstream of the OT tradition. The words "dust" and "turn" ("return") in v. 20 are the same ones used in Gen. 3:19. The Hebrew word *ruah* is translated in the RSV as "breath" in Eccl. 3:19 and as "spirit" in v. 21. The different renderings obscure the fact that most OT witnesses see no real difference between the breath of life and "the spirit." Both humans and animals were thought to depend on the LORD for the breath which gave them life (e.g., Gen. 2:7; Ps. 104:29-30).

In the final analysis Qohelet says it all comes down to this: we cannot *know* what will come "after" our lives under the sun are over. So, Qohelet concludes, we might as well enjoy what work we have been given to do (Eccl. 3:22) and (by implication in this context) leave whatever comes "after" (whether it be reward or punishment) in God's hands. This argument will be reintroduced and reconsidered in ch. 8 with even more of an emphasis on the inability of human beings to "find out what God has done."

CHAPTER FOUR

REPRISE (4:1-3)

The discussion of earthly rewards begun in 3:16 continues here in 4:1-3. Again Qohelet argues with proverbial wisdom when he refers to his own experiences. The wise may have believed that the LORD would protect and uphold the righteous (e.g., Prov. 10:3, 29), but Qohelet has seen "the oppressions that are practiced under the sun," and it is clear to him that the oppressed have not been "comforted" on a regular basis (Eccl. 4:1). Again, he confesses that when he realized that his retributive beliefs were contradicted in experience, he reacted at first with depression: "I thought the dead who are already dead more fortunate than the living who are still alive." The living have to face the disturbing reality of all the evil that is done "under the sun" (vv. 2-3).

TO WORK OR NOT TO WORK . . . (4:4-6)

In the RSV v. 4 is translated as if it were a conclusion drawn from the reasoning in vv. 1-3 ("then I saw . . ."). But in Hebrew the literal sense of "and I saw . . ." marks a change of subject, from that of injustice back to the topic of work or "toil." Both v. 4 and v. 6 give a negative valuation to excessive work. Verse 4 asserts that hard work done out of envy for one's neighbor is *hebel*, and v. 6 declares that "a handful of quietness" is better than "two hands full of toil" towards an unreachable goal. However, v. 5 tempers what might otherwise seem to be absolute claims. In what appears to be a traditional proverb, someone (either a glossator or Qohelet himself) reminds us that failure or refusal to work at all can have negative consequences, too. Excessive toil may be foolish and counterproductive, but we are also fools if we fold our hands and starve to death. Again the partial nature of proverbial truths

164

becomes evident in the text. In Qohelet's opinion neither the proverbial "sluggard" nor the compulsive worker trying to outshine his or her neighbor is worthy of emulation.

ON COMPANIONSHIP (4:7-12)

As it now stands, v. 7 seems incomplete: it serves only as a heading for v. 8 in which Qohelet gives an example of what he means by the *hebel* quality of working to pile up riches. This ancient description of an individual who has no living heir but who works hard and lives frugally in order to amass wealth resonates with reality in the contemporary world. Again, in Qohelet's opinion, the accumulation of wealth is not an adequate reason for depriving oneself of the simpler pleasures in life. The energies of the solitary miser would be put to better use in looking for companionship, in finding someone with whom to share the rewards of his labors.

In accord with these sentiments, vv. 9-12 list some of the advantages of living in community: support (v. 10), warmth (v. 11), and strength (v. 12). The concluding statement in v. 12, "a threefold cord is not quickly broken," has the aura of a traditional proverb. Apparently some activities are less *hebel* than others, in Qohelet's experience. Working to achieve community seems to promise more lasting rewards than simply working to become rich.

KINGSHIP TOO WILL PASS (4:13-16)

The strength of the threefold cord (v. 12) may refer to more than mere physical strength. The advantages of being in real community with others include being able to benefit from the wisdom of others. Qohelet does not stand in opposition to everything traditional wisdom advocates. The attitude Qohelet expresses in vv. 13-14 towards the taking of advice is identical with that found throughout the book of Proverbs. A primary characteristic of being wise is said to be the willingness to seek out and to take advice (e.g., Prov. 10:8; 12:15; 13:10). A wise king seeks out the best advisors available, because the strength of a government depends heavily upon the quantity and quality of sound advice its rulers are able to garner (e.g., Prov. 11:14; 20:18; 24:5-6). TEV seems to capture the sense of Eccl. 4:13-14 better than most translations: "A man may rise from poverty to become king of his country, or go from prison to the throne, but if in his old age he is too foolish to take advice, he is not as well off as a young man who is poor but intelligent."

In vv. 15-16 Qohelet reverts to his usual pattern of pointing out the partial nature of proverbial truths. A king's "glory" may depend on the number of people he rules, as Prov. 14:28 asserts, but Qohelet is convinced that no matter how many people are under a ruler's control, "those who come later will not rejoice in him" (Eccl. 4:16). This remark may either refer to the king's successors, who are waiting anxiously to replace him, or it may hark back to the earlier assertions in 1:11; 2:16, that human achievements cannot have an enduring impact on the future. Qohelet counters the proverbial awe shown towards the mighty powers of the king (e.g., Prov. 16:14-15) with a timely reminder. No matter how great a king's power in his own lifetime, both he and his kingship eventually will pass and will be forgotten.

Eccl. 4 ends with another ambiguous reference: "this also is *hebel* and a striving after wind." The antecedent of "this" could be the failure of those who "come later" to "rejoice in him," or it could refer to the phenomenon of a king who was wise enough to rise unexpectedly to power but not wise enough to continue to seek advice.

CHAPTER FIVE

FOOLISH FORMS OF RELIGIOSITY (5:1-7)

The reflective "journaling" style which characterizes the first four chapters of Ecclesiastes changes in 5:1 to a commanding or advice-giving form. Instead of telling us "I saw" or "I said" or "I considered," 5:1-2 and 4-6 are addressed to a masculine singular "you." There are two units of advice given here (vv. 1-2 and 4-6), and each set of commands is followed by a saying in proverbial form (vv. 3 and 7) which seems to comment on the advice given.

When you go to a house of worship, the unnamed person addressed in vv. 1-2 is told, it is better for you to listen and learn than to "offer the sacrifice of fools." Since the word translated here as "listen" can also be translated "obey," Qohelet's advice may resonate with Samuel's statement to Saul, "to obey [i.e., 'listen'] is better than sacrifice" (1 Sam. 15:22). However, the term "sacrifice of fools" is ambiguous in Hebrew as well as in English. It could literally mean ordinary sacrifices that are made by fools. But the context, with its emphasis on speaking rashly, indicates that the word "sacrifice" is used here figuratively to mean foolish verbosity. Fools who offer up wordy or insincere prayers "do not know that they are doing evil" (Eccl. 5:1; cf. Prov. 10:19). But it is really not necessary to try to impress God with a multitude of words. Instead, Qohelet says, keep the words you utter before God to a minimum, because "God is in heaven, and you upon earth" (Eccl. 5:2). As a reason this is rather obscure. Perhaps it implies that God is too exalted to be bothered by a lot of unnecessary babbling from earthbound mortals. Or perhaps it means that God in heaven is able to see what our needs are without hearing a lot of words from us about them.

The proverbial saying in v. 3 seems to equate the irrelevant and

167

extraneous details which often accompany dreams with the way a fool talks in "the house of God." The NJV captures the sense of this verse with its translation: "Just as dreams come with much brooding, so does foolish utterance come with much speech."

The second bit of advice (vv. 4-6) is closely related to the first and sounds very similar to Prov. 20:25. Qohelet says, "Do not get carried away with religious fervor, and do not make promises you cannot or do not intend to keep" (vv. 4-5). The "messenger" in v. 6 probably refers to a functionary sent to collect whatever was pledged. The last part of v. 6 seems to imply that God can be expected to take retributive action against those who make but do not keep their promises. If this is Qohelet speaking, rather than an editor or a glossator, then there may be a direct contradiction between 5:6 and 9:2. Again, a proverbial-type saying in 5:7 ends the unit, but its meaning is unclear. A final command is tacked onto the end of the proverb: "fear God" (or as the NIV puts it, "stand in awe of God"). The word "fear" here is the same as the one used so frequently in Proverbs with the sense of "having reverence," but the phrase sounds quite different with the substitution of the generic term "God" (literally, "the gods") for the proper name LORD.

HIERARCHICAL GREED (5:8-9)

Qohelet is a realist who has observed the way hierarchical systems often work to the disadvantage of the poor. "Do not be amazed," he tells his listener in v. 8, "when you see graft in high places." In a hierarchical system of government the poor are oppressed and their rights are denied to them, because at each level of authority officials are only concerned with pleasing those who are higher than they are. The RSV translation of v. 9 twists the sense of the Hebrew text. In reality the text reads "the profit of the land is [shared] by them all," using the Hebrew word *yitron* which means "profit" or "what is left over" (as in 1:3). The phrase means that all the officials, from the king on down, take a portion of the profits from the farmer's field. Thus, Qohelet's opinion of the source of poverty is the same as that expressed in Prov. 13:23 ("The fallow ground of the poor yields much food, but it is swept away through injustice"). Both Qohelet and the speaker in Prov. 13:23 refuse to allow sayings such as "He who tills his land will have plenty of bead" (Prov. 28:19) or "A slack hand causes poverty" (Prov. 10:4) to be universalized into absolute truths.

WHY EVEN TRY TO GET RICH? (5:10-17)

The rather cynical (though many would say realistic) observations about "trickle-down" economics in Eccl. 5:8-9 are followed by a series of proverbial-type sayings in vv. 10-12 and a short narrative in vv. 13-17 which all deal with the topic of piling up riches. According to v. 10, those who love money or wealth will never feel satisfied with what they have. "This" (either wealth itself or the love of it) is also *hebel,* "a breath" (v. 10). It is not something to lean on. It does not endure.

"When goods increase, they increase who eat them" (v. 11) may be another reason why those who love money are never satiated with it or with what it can buy. The more one has, the more it takes to hang on to it. After a certain point one who has accumulated excess wealth can do little with it other than look at it. The "surfeit of the rich" may also keep them from sleeping peacefully at night. Unlike the "laborer" (the servant, the slave, or the one who tills the soil), the rich may lay awake nights worrying about how to hang on to all of their possesions (v. 12).

You Can't Take It With You

The narrative in vv. 13-17 is introduced once more as a reflection of Qohelet's personal experiences. The term behind the RSV's "grievous evil" is difficult to translate, but probably means something less drastic than this English phrase implies. The early Greek translators understood the words to mean a "sickness," which is a better translation. Qohelet is speaking about a twisted or unhealthy attitude towards wealth. He says that he has seen people who have accumulated and hoarded up riches at great sacrifice to themselves, apparently hoping to pass their wealth on to their heirs, only to have their fortunes wiped out in a single bad venture (vv. 13-14). They, like all other mortals, must go to their graves as "naked" as they were when they came from their mothers' wombs, without anything concrete to show for all the hard work they have done (vv. 15-16). Their heirs will be none the richer for all the scrimping and saving they had done. Thus, Qohelet asks himself and his

169

listener(s), "What gain *[yitron]* has he" (v. 16) for all the time he spent slaving away "in much vexation and sickness and resentment?" (v. 17).

WORK FOR THE SHEER JOY OF IT (5:18-20)

The speaker thus comes back once more to the topic which has dominated the entire discussion so far. Qohelet wants us to consider how we human beings can most profitably spend the brief period of time we are allotted on earth, since (as his story in vv. 13-17 demonstrates) we cannot really count on anything being left over from all our labors. Once again (as in 2:24; 3:13) his own conclusion is that God has given us the ability to find enjoyment in our work. What is good for a human being to do is "to eat and drink and find enjoyment in all the toil with which one toils under the sun" (5:18).

So far Qohelet has argued that toiling painfully and miserably day after day simply for the purpose of accumulating wealth is useless. Wealth cannot be relied upon to endure (vv. 13-17), it cannot be taken with us when we die (3:19-21; 4:7-8), and it cannot be controlled by us after we are gone (2:18-21). Now he adds that the ability to be content with what you have in life and to find enjoyment in your work is a gift of God (5:19). Those who find joy in the daily activities of eating, drinking, and working will neither notice nor worry about the brevity of life (v. 20). The first section in ch. 6 will continue to argue along much the same lines.

CHAPTER SIX

WITHOUT THE POWER OF ENJOYMENT YOU HAVE NOTHING (6:1-6)

The RSV makes it difficult to see that the first six verses of the chapter all refer to the same hypothetical person, someone who has everything anyone's heart could desire—including wealth, possessions, and honor (v. 2), plus many children and a long life (v. 3). In various parts of Proverbs each of these things is said to be the result of living righteously and wisely. But if such a person does not have the ability to enjoy life's good things, says Qohelet, he or she is no better off than an aborted fetus or a stillborn child, which never sees the light or knows anything (vv. 4-5). It does not matter how long you live if you are not capable of enjoying what you have while you are alive (v. 6). At least one speaker in Proverbs agrees with Qohelet's point of view: "It is the blessing of the LORD that enriches, and no toil can increase it" (Prov. 10:22 NJV).

The train of thought in Eccl. 6:1-6 is interrupted (or at least made more complicated) by a comment in v. 3 that appears to be an afterthought or a gloss. It was a common belief in the ancient Near East that a decent burial was a precondition for the deceased to be able to rest peacefully in the realm of the dead. Thus, the comment about burial in v. 3 is probably related to the statement about finding "rest" in v. 5. The statement that a "premature (RSV 'untimely') birth" would find "rest" while one who "has no burial" would not is superimposed over the basic train of thought in vv. 1-6. It may represent some later reader's attempt to understand Qohelet's claim that a stillborn child could be considered better off in many ways than someone who had lived a long and prosperous life.

Once again, it seems Qohelet is arguing that the power of

171

enjoyment is the only thing we can own that is truly our own. Everything else must be passed on to someone else when we die (v. 2). The rhetorical question in v. 6 apparently expects the answer "Yes, of course, we all know that everyone goes to 'the same place.'" The prevailing traditions in Israel undoubtedly thought of the grave (or Sheol) as the destination for all mortal beings (e.g., 3:19-20; Gen. 3:19), and Qohelet makes no attempt to argue with this understanding.

A WRAP-UP OF CHS. 1–6 (6:7-12)

The final six verses of Eccl. 6 repeat significant themes from previous chapters and act as both a conclusion to the first half and an introduction to the second half of the book. (See comments in the Introduction to Ecclesiastes, above.)

The catch phrase "this also is *hebel* and a striving after wind" occurs for the last time in 6:9. Presumably "this" refers to one or more of the things named in vv. 7-9. The proverbial-type utterance in v. 7 refers once again to the question of what motivates people to work hard. There is a resemblance between this saying and Prov. 16:26 ("A worker's appetite works for him; his mouth urges him on"). However, Qohelet's version asserts that while we work for things which can be consumed, we find that such things are not ultimately satisfying. Just as "all streams run to the sea, but the sea is not full" (Eccl. 1:7), or as "the eye is not satisfied with seeing, nor the ear filled with hearing" (1:8), so our human endeavors are all directed towards "our mouths," but our "appetites" are never satisfied. The words "to be full" in 1:7 and "to be satisfied" in 6:7 are the same. The word translated "appetite" in 6:7 is also translated "desire" in v. 9; but Hebrew *nephesh,* meaning the "whole person" or the "inner person," would be better translated as "self" in both places. Thus, Eccl. 6:7 seems to agree with Deut. 8:3—human beings cannot really "live" by what they put in their mouths alone.

The word "advantage" in Eccl. 6:8 comes from the same root as the word "profit" or "gain." The question asked in v. 8 has in mind the same point as 2:13-16. Is there any ultimate advantage in working hard to become wise or to learn how to conduct oneself properly in life? The answer given in 6:9 is in essence the same as that given in 2:14. Yes, it is better to have seeing eyes (i.e., be wise) than to "walk in darkness" (2:14) or to have what RSV calls "the

172

wandering of desire" as fools do. But both the "sight" of the wise and the "wandering" of the foolish are "like a breath" (transitory). In other words Qohelet thinks it is better to be wise than to be foolish. But he recognizes that in the long run neither the wise nor the foolish have anything more substantial to show for their endeavors than they would if they tried to grasp hold of the wind.

The first half of 6:10 recalls the assertion made in 1:9-11 that there is "nothing new under the sun." The second half of the verse may suggest a matter-of-fact acceptance of the knowledge that humans cannot contend with God or act counter to God's plans (although the word "God" does not appear here). This seems to have been the implication in 1:15; 3:14, and this was the viewpoint frequently expressed in Proverbs (e.g., Prov. 19:21; 21:30-31).

The first half of the book of Ecclesiastes concludes with an assertion that there is nothing to be gained by continuing to talk on the topic of work (Eccl. 6:11). The second half of the book is then introduced by the two questions in v. 12. The first of these, "Who knows what is good [for humans to do while they live out the days of their breathlike lives]?" is the same question Qohelet asked in 2:3, when he was considering various reasons for diligence and hard work. But in the remaining chapters of the book, we will no longer be concerned with the topic of "work." In the following chapters the emphasis in the question being considered shifts from the word "do" to the words "good" and "know."

Our attention will be directed in most of the upcoming chapters towards the topic of human knowledge and its boundaries. The second question, "Who can tell . . . ?" hints at the doubt Qohelet has concerning the extent to which we human beings can "know" anything about what comes after us "under the sun." The catch-words which occur in the second half of the book are based on the roots for "know," "tell," and "find out."

CHAPTER SEVEN

The second half of the book of Ecclesiastes begins with a series of proverbial observations that all have to do with the question "What is good?" (In Hebrew "better" is literally "more good than"). Much of the subject matter in ch. 7 is echoed both in Proverbs and elsewhere in Ecclesiastes. The first twelve verses, in particular, are similar in both form and content to the Solomonic sayings, though Qohelet occasionally adds an ironic twist to suit his own purposes. The emphasis that characterized the first six chapters (on the amount of effort wasted in the accumulation of consumer goods) is not forgotten, but now it becomes the background against which several new themes stand out.

ENDS ARE BETTER THAN BEGINNINGS (7:1-4, 8)

Five sayings in ch. 7 make observations about the reality of death and our reactions to it. The beginning of v. 1 agrees with Prov. 22:1 that a good reputation is of more value to its owner than the things money can buy. In Hebrew the saying is a play on similar-sounding words, making it "catchy" to the ear as well as to the mind. Few would disagree with its initial valuation. But the saying ends with a cryptic twist: "and the day of death [is better than] the day of birth." Like many proverbial utterances, such an observation could take on a variety of meanings, depending on the context in which it was said. Used at a funeral, the saying could reflect on the fulfillment of a life's potential. At the day of birth no one knows what a child will do or become "under the sun." But on the day of death, all that can be known is known. And if what is known adds up to "a good name," indicating a life well spent, then what is left behind is of more value than "precious ointment." The emphasis of the saying could also be placed on the length of time something

174

lasts. Being given a good "name" on the day of your birth is not worth much unless the rest of your life sustains it. But if you have a good "name" on the day of your death, it will endure longer than even the most expensive perfume.

This is also the sentiment expressed in the first half of Eccl. 7:8: "Better is the end of a thing than its beginning." The word which the RSV translates "end" here seems to mean "the latter part of life" in Prov. 14:12; 25:8 but is translated "future" in Prov. 23:18; 24:14, 20. The English word "completion" might have been a better choice than "end" in the first part of Eccl. 7:8. Then it would be easier to see that the completion of a "thing" (a task or an affair) is tied to the "patience" which is praised in the second half of the verse. However, an entirely different Hebrew word lies beneath the translation "end" in v. 2. The saying in v. 2 refers to the cutting off of life rather than to its completion. The difference in the words for "end" may be simply a matter of perspective. Looking back on someone else's life, we can see the sense in which it is complete. But contemplating the fact of another's death can also prompt us to consider how quickly our own lives may come to an "end." Thus, the saying in v. 2 asserts that the living can learn more from attending a funeral (going to "the house of mourning") than from celebrating the birth of a baby (going to "the house of feasting"). Going to a funeral should prompt the living to reflect on how quickly life can come to an end.

The sayings in vv. 3-4 simply continue the train of thought begun in vv. 1-2. We should not universalize these proverbial observations. In all of the rest of Ecclesiastes, Qohelet praises joy and the enjoyment of life in spite of its ephemeral nature. Here he recommends the contemplation of the fact of death, not in a morbid sense but as a way of persuading his audience that life is too short to be wasted. The contemplation of sorrow (v. 3) and mourning (vv. 2 and 4) should be done so that "the heart is made glad" (v. 3) while there is yet time for the living to do so. It is wiser to remember that life is short (because remembering helps us to cherish it) than foolishly to think and act as if there were no end to our personal existence. All of the previous illustrations concerning those who spend their lives in a frenetic scramble to accumulate riches or wisdom act as an introduction to what is said in vv. 1-4 and 8. This material is still addressed to the workaholics who have been the subject of previous passages.

BETTER WISE THAN FOOLISH WAYS (7:5-10)

A play on words (the juxtapositioning of Hebrew *shir* ["song"] with *sir* ["pot"] and *sirrim* ["thorns"]) indicates that vv. 5-6 belong together. The belief that those who are wise are open to rebuke and those who are foolish are not is commonly expressed in Proverbs (e.g., Prov. 15:12, 31). Here it is said that it is better to be rebuked by the wise than praised by fools (cf. Prov. 27:5). Again, as in the reflections on death, Qohelet is concerned with what gives us the greatest benefit. Foolish laughter is about as much use as thorns are beneath the pot (lots of noise, little heat). Both are *hebel* (of short duration).

In the RSV Eccl. 7:7 is ambiguous. It is not oppression directed against the wise but oppression which they direct against others which makes the wise foolish. Qohelet observes that taking bribes not only results in a miscarriage of justice (as Prov. 17:23 also noted), it also "corrupts the mind" and turns the wise person into a fool.

The first part of Eccl. 7:8 was discussed above in conjunction with the sayings on death in vv. 1-4. But the second section of v. 8 is linked to v. 9 by the threefold repetition in Hebrew of the word *ruah* (translated in v. 8 as "spirit."). The translation "quick to anger" in v. 9 represents the Hebrew idiom "hasty in spirit," so that taken together the two verses commend the "patient in spirit" and condemn both "the proud in spirit" and "the hasty in spirit" in much the same way as do the Solomonic sayings (e.g., Prov. 12:16; 14:29; 16:32; 29:23).

"Say not, 'Why were the former days better than these?'" Qohelet advises us in Eccl. 7:10. If "there is nothing new under the sun" (1:9), then there is no such thing as "the good old days" either. The wise know that the present is neither better nor worse than the past.

WILL WISDOM AND WEALTH PROTECT YOU? (7:11-12, 19)

In previous passages Qohelet argued that wealth was easily lost (5:13-17) and was not a very dependable source of satisfaction (4:7-8; 5:10). He concluded that wise and foolish people alike have the same fate (2:14-16). Now however, he adds that wisdom combined with an inheritance is "an advantage to those who see the sun" (7:11). Although neither wisdom nor wealth can shield you from the inevitability of death, wisdom can help prolong the period of time you spend "under the sun" (v. 12b). Whether you see the first part of v. 12 as an ironic or a serious statement probably depends on how you understood Prov. 18:10-11. But if any consistency of viewpoint is assumed and if the preceding passages in Eccl. 1–6 are taken seriously, then 7:12a must mean that neither wisdom nor money are ultimately dependable. Wisdom and wealth are definitely preferable to folly and poverty, and wisdom is definitely stronger than any protection money can buy (v. 19; cf. Prov. 24:5). Nevertheless, the protection offered by either wisdom or money is relatively flimsy, compared with the power of God.

GOD IS IN CONTROL (7:13-18)

The conclusion that Qohelet rates the "protection" of anything under the sun fairly low is strengthened by Eccl. 7:13-14. In v. 13 a repetition of the saying already used in 1:15 functions as a reminder that God is in ultimate control and that we humans cannot change ("make straight") anything God has done. The best we can do, if we are wise, is to enjoy prosperity when we have it and to endure "the day of adversity" when it comes, reflecting on God's purposes for making either one happen.

Qohelet has reflected, he has applied his considerable intellect to the problem, and 7:14 implies that he has decided that God brings both prosperity and adversity—not as reward or punishment for human behavior but as a way to keep human beings from finding out "anything that will be after" them (v. 14). In 3:22; 6:12 Qohelet merely questioned the possibility of our knowing what "comes after" us "under the sun." Here in 7:14 he asserts that God deliberately keeps us from such knowledge.

Some readers think that Qohelet is accusing God of having a petty need to keep humans under control by denying them insight into the future. But I would argue that it is in fact the concept of grace which undergirds Qohelet's argument. Human beings who think they know precisely what God is about often fall prey to the conceit that they can earn God's favor. But Qohelet argues that God keeps us ignorant about the future in order to convince us that we cannot manipulate God in that way. That is the essence of what it means to "fear" God: to recognize that God's favor cannot be controlled by anything we humans can do.

177

As evidence to support his conclusion that there is no way for us to guarantee that our righteous behavior will bring us rewards or that wicked behavior will bring punishment, Qohelet refers in v. 15 to his own observations of reality. In his own brief life Qohelet has seen that the righteous do sometimes "perish" in the midst of their righteousness and the wicked do sometimes manage to "prolong" their lives in or through their evildoing (v. 15). Since this is the case, Qohelet offers two bits of advice to the reader. On the one hand he says, "Be not righteous overmuch, and do not make yourself overwise" (v. 16). No matter how piously or righteously you act, you will not be able to guarantee your prosperity. On the other hand, "Be not wicked overmuch, neither be a fool" (v. 17). Overzealousness toward either extreme can have negative consequences. Qohelet apparently believes that if you act without moderation, you risk either destroying yourself or dying "before your time" (vv. 16-17). But it is clear that he does not consider these consequences to be mediated by God.

The Hebrew in the last part of v. 18 is very difficult to understand, as a brief survey of major translations will indicate. Most versions agree that the first part of the verse asserts that it is good to do different things—to take hold of or to hold on to some (unspecified) things and not to lose hold of or not to let go of other things. But ways of understanding what it says that the person who fears God will do vary. The RSV reads "shall come forth from them all," while the NAB has "will win through at all events," the NJV translates "will do his duty by both," and the NIV has "will avoid all [extremes]."

In 3:14 Qohelet claimed that the "fear" of God was related to humanity's inability to comprehend or to alter the totality of what God has done. Here in 7:13-18 there seems to be a similar progression of thought from our powerlessness to alter God's works (v. 13) to our inherent ignorance of the future (v. 14). Thus, the person who "fears God" (v. 18) is probably thought of as one who knows that the future (which God controls) truly cannot be known to humankind. Those who fear God will do what needs to be done, as human wisdom advises (v. 19), without presuming they *know* what will come forth from it all, without presuming that they will be able to manipulate God into bestowing "blessings" upon them.

178

NOBODY IS PERFECT (7:20-29)

A new topic is introduced in v. 20 with a saying which resembles
Prov. 20:9. The blanket statement in Eccl. 7:20 acts as rationale for
the advice given in v. 21. Since we all make mistakes from time to
time, we ought to take what other people say about us with the
proverbial grain of salt.

In vv. 23-29 Qohelet tells us that he has tried to use wisdom to
find out the scheme or "the sum of things," (v. 25) but he has come
to the conclusion that kind of knowledge "is far off, and deep, very
deep" (v. 24). The question "who can find it out?" implies that no
one can. Some things can be discovered by wisdom, however. In
the process of his futile search for the overall plan or "sum" of all
things, Qohelet "found" *something* "more bitter than death." The
RSV says that Qohelet found "the woman whose heart is snares
and nets, and whose hands are fetters" (v. 26). In spite of the way
the text has sometimes been used, it is clear that Qohelet is not
accusing women in general of entrapment tendencies. If we ask
who "the woman" is who best fits this description, we might easily
find an answer in the personification of Folly in Prov. 9:13-18. As
in Proverbs the one who pleases God is said to be able to escape
from the nets of folly, "but the sinner is taken by her" (Eccl. 7:26).

The second half of v. 28 is obscure in the Hebrew, and the RSV
renders it quite literally and accurately. Translations which try to
add further clarity (such as the NIV's "I found one [upright] man
among a thousand, but not one [upright] woman among them
all") have no textual basis for their guesswork. However, Qohelet's conclusion in v. 29 is quite lucid. There is a wordplay in vv.
25, 27, and 29 based on two different senses of the same word,
which RSV translates "sum" in vv. 25 and 27 and "devices" in
v. 29. The word "scheme" is the best English equivalent for this
one Hebrew word (as NIV recognizes), because in English
"scheme" can also be understood in two ways, either meaning "an
overall plan" or "devious plans." Qohelet says that he has tried to
use wisdom to find "the scheme of things" but all he could
discover was that human beings are all "schemers" (in spite of the
fact that God created them "upright"). In other words we are back
to the theme expressed in 3:10, 14; 7:14 that mortals, for all their
clever attempts to do so, cannot find out what God has in store
for them.

CHAPTER EIGHT

The exploration of the theme of the boundaries of human wisdom continues with the questions "who knows?" and "who can tell?" in 8:1 and 7 and the assertions "does not know," "will not find it out," and "cannot find (it) out" in vv. 7 and 17.

WHAT WISDOM CAN AND CANNOT KNOW (8:1-9)

Qohelet tells us that by applying his mind "to all that is done under the sun" (v. 9) he has been able to observe where wisdom is and where it is not effective. On the one hand, wisdom can help a person make practical choices in life-threatening situations. In 7:12 Qohelet suggested that wisdom can "preserve the life" of the wise. To "preserve life" (literally, "keep alive") means simply to prolong one's life span within natural limits. Thus, in 8:2-5 Qohelet illustrates one of the ways wisdom can function to help the wise avoid a premature demise. When the king to whom you have sworn loyalty commands you to do something, Qohelet says, you have to do it even if it is distasteful to you (vv. 2-3). No one can question the king's orders (v. 4), but wisdom will help you to "know the time and way" to make the best of a bad situation (v. 5). On the other hand, Qohelet seems to say in v. 6-9, there is a sense in which no one can really know what the consequences of a given action will be. Even though one human being continues to "lord it over" another (v. 9), even such despots as the king have no real "power to retain the spirit, or authority over the day of death" (v. 8). The idea that one cannot determine either one's own or another's "day of death" will occur again in v. 12.

The phrase in v. 8 which the RSV translates "there is no discharge from war" should be understood in the context to mean there is no release from the battle or the struggle in which all

180

mortals are engaged. Even wickedness cannot release us from our
uncertainty about the future.

In this passage Qohelet continues to affirm (as he did in ch. 3)
that there really is an appropriate time and an appropriate way to
deal with everything under the sun. But at the same time he
observes that our troubles weigh heavily upon us because no one
(no matter how wise or how wicked) can *know* for sure what is yet
to come. The word translated "way" in 8:5-6 is *mishpat,* meaning
"judgment," or the process of making a decision. Qohelet says that
there is a proper decision to make in every case, but even the wisest
of us cannot tell what it is in advance (v. 7; see also Commentary
on 7:14).

A passage in the Egyptian Instruction of Amenemope reflects a
similar point of view: "Do not spend the night fearful of the
morrow. . . . Man knows not what the morrow is like" (xix.10ff.;
ANET, 423).

When Reality Contradicts Tradition (8:10-15)

Once again, as in 3:16-22, Qohelet struggles to come to terms
with the failure of traditional beliefs to explain the realities experienced in human life. And again, as was the case in ch. 3, Qohelet
follows his affirmations of faith with reflections on how far the
realities of human experience vary from the ideal. He himself has
seen that the wicked who "used to go in and out of the holy place"
are often buried with much praise from people who knew what evil
things they had done (8:10). He has also seen that the failure to
punish evildoers tempts others to follow in their footsteps (v. 11).
But he still is convinced that "it will be well with those who fear
God, because they fear before him" (v. 12) and that "it will not be
well with the wicked" (v. 13).

Verse 13 can be understood in two different ways. Qohelet may
be affirming that the refusal of the wicked to "fear before God" will
result in a reduction of their life span ("the wicked will not prolong
their days"). This would then be a statement completely in line
with the wisdom opinions expressed in Prov. 10:27 or 13:9.
However, if the verse is read this way, then there is a definite
contradiction between Eccl. 8:13 and the first part of v. 12
("Though a sinner does evil a hundred times and prolongs his
life . . .").

181

Verse 13 could also be read as being in agreement with v. 8. It is possible that both v. 8 and v. 13 make the same affirmation. Some people in Qohelet's audience may have suggested that in the "real world" the wicked actually have an advantage over the righteous. But Qohelet declares that wickedness cannot "deliver those who are given to it" (v. 8). And in v. 13 he denies the possibility that the refusal to fear before God might even *lengthen* the sinner's life (i.e., the wicked will not prolong their days by refusing to fear before God).

But even if this is the case, Qohelet has to admit that, contrary to tradition (e.g., Prov. 10:27), sinning does not appear to shorten the life of the wicked either (Eccl. 8:12)! In fact no matter what the wise profess to believe (e.g., Prov. 10:2, 16; 11:4), the evidence of Qohelet's eyes indicates to him that "on earth" there are righteous people "to whom it happens according to the deeds of the wicked," and there are wicked people "to whom it happens according to the deeds of the righteous" (v. 14). This, too, Qohelet concludes, is *hebel*.

Interpreters have tried in a variety of ways to explain the apparent contradiction between the affirmation "I know that it will be well with those who fear God" in v. 12 and the observation in v. 14 that this is not what actually happens "on earth." Some suggest that Qohelet is simply quoting the tradition in order to refute it. Thus, TEV inserts "Oh yes, I know what they say . . ." into v. 12, to indicate that Qohelet is disassociating himself with what "they" say. Others think that vv. 12-13 were added by later pious editors who wanted to make the words of Qohelet more "acceptable" within the tradition.

However, if the word *hebel* is understood literally as a metaphor meaning "a breath" or figuratively meaning "of short duration," then there is no need to assume either that the argument is inconsistent or that the original text has been amended. Here in ch. 8, as was the case in ch. 3, Qohelet first denies that retribution takes place "under the sun" and then affirms that this is a "breath," a temporary state of affairs. In both chs. 3 and 8 the juxtapositioning of the ideal ("I said in my heart" in 3:17-18 and "I know" in 8:12) with the real ("I saw" in 8:10 and in 3:16) is followed by a recommendation of what is good for us humans to do while this temporary state of affairs lasts: eat, drink, and enjoy your work during the brief life God gives you "under the sun" (8:15 and 3:22).

182

The exact same Hebrew words are used in 3:12 and 8:15, but for some unexplained reason the RSV translates "there is nothing better for [humanity] than" in 3:12 and "[humanity] has no good thing . . . but" in 8:15. Since other sections of the book have clearly stated that the ability to enjoy these breathlike pleasures is a gift from God (2:24-26; 3:13; 6:2), the translation of 8:15 (which implies that this is a sad alternative) is unjustifiable. This is the counsel of wisdom, not of despair, and the answer Qohelet gives to the question of what is good for humans to do during their brief lives under the sun is quite a cheerful one. Qohelet says "I commend enjoyment," because he values it as the most durable and valuable result of human endeavors.

 ## THERE ARE LIMITS TO WHAT YOU CAN KNOW
(8:16-17)

In v. 16 Qohelet returns to the first person "journaling" or reflective style which characterized earlier passages. Once again he focuses his attention on the futility of working to try to know everything there is to be known on earth. Qohelet does not disparage the acquisition of knowledge in and for itself. Learning is undoubtedly a good thing in his opinion but not, he insists, if it is pursued obsessively (so that "neither day nor night one's eyes see sleep"). The editor who adds 12:12 to the end of Qohelet's works seems to agree with this point of view.

Qohelet's deliberations have convinced him that it is impossible for anyone to comprehend "all the work of God." No matter how hard you work to find out everything God has done, you "will not find it out." Even if someone claims to know, the truth is that a human being "cannot find it out" (v. 17). This is both the way it is and the way God wants it to be. The topic of the limits of human wisdom which was first introduced in ch. 3 is thus repeated and elaborated in ch. 8 and forms a basis for the meditations with which ch. 9 begins.

The thread of logic which runs throughout the second half of Ecclesiastes is spun from Qohelet's conviction that human beings must live out their lives without being able to find out precisely what God has in mind to do. Mortals must run the risk of choosing to act without knowing what the ultimate results of their actions will be.

CHAPTER NINE

Qohelet tells us that he laid "all this" to heart (referring back, perhaps, to 8:16-17), examining or exploring the idea that "the righteous and the wise and their deeds are in the hand of God." His meditations lead him to conclude that human beings cannot know what lies before them, "whether it is love or hate (9:1).

ONE FATE COMES TO ALL (9:2-6)

However, there is one thing about the future that we all know, muses Qohelet. We know that sooner or later all living creatures will die. In 3:18-21 Qohelet had considered whether or not there was any observable difference between what happens to animals and what happens to humans after they die. At that point he concluded that as far as we humans can tell, the breath of life (or the "spirit") is the same in both. Now Qohelet turns his attention to different types of human beings. The evidence seems to him to indicate that whether they live in righteous or in wicked ways, whether or not they have hearts full of evil and madness, all human beings will eventually join "the dead" (9:3). This, says Qohelet, is a problem (RSV "evil") from which we cannot escape "under the sun."

Qohelet includes a popular proverb ("a living dog is better than a dead lion") in his meditations (v. 4), and he echoes ideas about death that are common in the traditions of Israel. The inevitability of death presents us with a problem, Qohelet seems to say, because as far as we can tell, "the dead know nothing," apparently "they have no more reward," and even "the memory of them is lost" (v. 5). From a purely empirical point of view, the dead "have no more for ever any share in all that is done under the sun" (v. 6). Again there is a parallel between the understanding of death

184

presented here and in 3:20 ("all are from the dust, and all turn to dust again").

Some interpreters think 9:2-6 represents Qohelet's reasoned conclusions on the subject of death. Others point to the first verse ("all this I laid to heart") as evidence that Qohelet is still debating the issues within himself. I suggest that Qohelet is still weighing the evidence of his senses over against traditions which have been handed down for generations in his community of faith. And the conclusion he reaches, based on the traditional viewpoint, is expressed in the next section (vv. 7-10).

ENJOY YOUR PORTION IN LIFE (9:7-10)

Qohelet's true opinion seems to me to be that we humans cannot *know* for sure "what comes after" our lives under the sun. But in this section he seems to say to his audience, "Even if you are totally convinced that 'there is no work or thought or knowledge or wisdom in Sheol, to which you are going,' you should still put the time you have been allotted under the sun to good use" (9:10). In the previous chapter he commended enjoyment even when he saw that reality did not live up to traditional expectations (8:14-15). Here his advice to those who think they know what the future will be like remains the same. Enjoy what you have to eat, to drink, and to wear. Enjoy married life and throw yourself energetically (but joyfully) into whatever work needs to be done (9:10). And once again (as in 2:24; 3:13; 5:19), Qohelet asserts that this (enjoying the everyday aspects of life) is what God wants us to do (9:7).

TIME AND CHANCE HAPPEN TO ALL (9:11-12)

Again Qohelet uses personal experience as a standard by which to measure the truth of traditional teachings. It is simply not true, in his experience ("Again I saw") that those who do well receive their just deserts "under the sun." Contrary to popular opinion, the race is not always won by the swiftest runner, the battle is not always won by the strongest participant. The wise, the clever, and the intelligent do not always succeed in their endeavors. And contrary to proverbial wisdom, which seems to think that you can do things guaranteed to lengthen or to shorten your life span (e.g., Prov. 10:27; 13:9; 11:4), Qohelet asserts that the time of death is unpredictable. It falls upon us like a net or a snare without warning. Whether or not we succeed in our endeavors and whether death comes to us early or late is simply a matter of "time and chance."

WISDOM IS BETTER THAN WEAPONS, BUT . . .
(9:13-18)

Qohelet is fully convinced of the desirability of wisdom. But he wants his audience to recognize that wisdom also has its limitations. When Qohelet tells this brief story of a city saved from destruction by the wisdom of one insignificant person, he does not contradict the proverbs which exalt wisdom over physical strength or military might (e.g., Prov. 24:5; 21:22). In fact he continues to say that "wisdom is better than might" (Eccl. 9:16). But the point that he makes through the story he tells is that even this spectacular achievement did not make the wise person immortal. Contrary to the expectations expressed in Prov. 10:7, Qohelet insists that no one remembered the poor man's name (Eccl 9:15). However, recognizing the limitations of wisdom does not erase the fact that wisdom is "better than weapons of war" (vv. 18) and better than "the shouting of a ruler among fools" (v. 17). The chapter closes with an ambiguous reference to the damage one "sinner" can do (v. 18). The antecedent for the word "sinner" could be the shouting ruler in v. 17, but it is more likely that the phrase is used here in a generalized sense. Since the word translated "sin" means literally "to miss the mark" or "to make a mistake," v. 18 may mean that one person who makes a mistake can destroy much of the good wisdom does. The following verse (10:1) expresses the same idea (that it only takes a little folly to outweigh wisdom). Thus, the entire section (9:13-18) is concerned with both the strengths and the limitations of wisdom.

CHAPTER TEN

The person who summarizes Qohelet's career for us in the conclusion to the book of Ecclesiastes claims that besides being wise, Qohelet "also taught the people knowledge, weighing and studying and arranging proverbs with great care" (12:9). Chapter 10 seems to contain an arrangement of such proverbs, most of which resemble either the Solomonic sayings or sections of the "Words of the Wise" collections in the book of Proverbs. Only Eccl. 10:1, 5-7, and 14-15 are concerned with the previous subjects of Qohelet's meditations.

FOLLY ACCORDING TO QOHELET (10:1-3, 5-7, 12-15)

The first verse in the chapter picks up on a previously quoted proverb and uses it to make one more comment on the topic of the limitations of wisdom. "A good name" may well be "better than precious ointment," as the proverb in 7:1 said, but Qohelet also says that a little folly can spoil the work or the reputation of the wise as fast as flies can make an ointment "give off an evil odor" (10:1).

The comments that are made about fools in vv. 2-3 and 12-13 resemble Solomonic sayings in both form and content. Verse 2 is expressed in antithetical parallelism, a form which is frequently found in Proverbs but seldom occurs in the rest of Ecclesiastes. Verse 3 seems to manifest more contempt for the fool than most of the sayings in Proverbs did, implying that absolutely everything the fool does proclaims his folly (something like "you can see one coming a mile away").

In vv. 5-7 Qohelet tells us of another phenomenon he has observed "under the sun." Sometimes "folly is set in many high places, and the rich sit in a low place" (v. 6). Once again his

187

eyesight provides him with an illustration that the rewards which tradition encourages us to expect are not guaranteed. Reality often confronts us with a reversal of our expectations so that we find "slaves on horses, and princes walking on foot like slaves" (v. 7; cf. Prov. 19:10; 11:29b). There are no guarantees under the sun!

Two Solomonic-type sayings about fools in Eccl. 10:12-13 are used to reintroduce one of Qohelet's favorite topics. Qohelet says that fools begin by talking about foolishness and end up talking about "wicked madness" (v. 13). And one example of such madness, in Qohelet's opinion, is continuing to talk on the subject of the future even though no one knows "what is to be" (v. 14). Fools work so hard at this futile exercise that they forget even the simplest of things, like how to get to town (v. 15).

RULERS AND KINGS (10:4, 16-20)

The sayings in v. 4 and v. 20 advise those who have to deal with rulers to exercise extreme caution and self-control in much the same way as Prov. 16:14-15 or 25:6-7 gave advice about prudent behavior in the presence of the king. But Eccl. 10:16-17 is addressed (ostensibly) to the land rather than to an individual. The word which the RSV translates "child" in v. 16 also means a household servant or a personal retainer (as in 2 Kgs. 4:12). Since the following verse refers to the free born (or nobles, as in 1 Kgs. 21:8), the contrast between the two kings mentioned in Eccl. 10:16-17 is probably one of status or family background rather than age. However, the emphasis here is not elitist. It is not the "royal blood" which is praised in v. 17, but the ability of the king to keep the "feasting" of his "princes" under control. Again, as was often the case in the book of Proverbs, the stability and the prosperity of the land is traced back to the responsible behavior of those who rule over it (e.g., Prov. 16:12: 20:28).

In spite of his many commendations of enjoyment, it is clear that Qohelet would never agree that simply "anything goes." Even eating and drinking, which he frequently urges us to enjoy, should be done "at the proper time" (the word used here is the same as in Eccl. 3:1-8) and should never be done to excess (i.e., feasting should be done for "strength," and not for "drunkenness," 10:17).

The sayings in vv. 18-19 may have originated as popular proverbs, but in their present position they could be understood as further comments on what happens to a land when it is *not* ruled wisely. Just as it is true that failure to do regular maintenance will result in a leaky house, it is also true that a king's "sloth" or "indolence" will weaken his "house." In a well-managed kingdom, eating and drinking are done "for strength" (v. 17), but the proverb in v. 19 may be commenting on the improper use of such things as bread, wine, and money. Because of the context in which we now find the verse and because Qohelet has so often expressed contempt for those who think that money is everything, I suggest that v. 19 is now being used as an illustration of the types of mismanagement which might tempt someone into cursing the king. The king or the rich who act as if "money answers everything" may deserve to be cursed, but v. 20 counsels the prudent not to put such thoughts into words.

MISCELLANEOUS MAXIMS (10:8-11)

The first half of v. 8 and the first half of Prov. 26:27 are identical. There is also a great deal of resemblance between the second half of Prov. 26:27 and the first half of Eccl. 10:9. Both the proverb and the sayings in vv. 8-9 are concerned with what might be called "poetic justice." This, however, is an opinion which Qohelet elsewhere says is contradicted in fact (e.g., 9:11-12).

The comment in 10:10 does not seem to be connected by content or form with vv. 8-9. Having wisdom is likened to having a sharp edge on an axe: it reduces the effort one needs to expend and increases one's chances of success. However v. 11 may also be a comment on the efficacy of wisdom: to be helpful, it has to be used at the right time.

CHAPTER ELEVEN

You Do Not Know What Will Prosper (11:1-6)

What does it mean to "cast your bread upon the waters?" Some readers interpret this figurative language in mercenary terms. Thus, TEV renders 11:1 as "Invest your money in foreign trade, and one of these days you will make a profit," and the NEB says, "Send your grain across the seas, and in time you will get a return." Some think it refers to an agricultural practice (such as broadcast sowing), and others have interpreted it in terms of charity or good deeds. Whatever the original sense of the idiom, in the context of vv. 1-6 it becomes a part of the theme which has dominated the entire second half of Qohelet's journal: "you do not know" what the future will bring (see the phrase "not know" in vv. 2, 5a, 5b, 6).

From a human perspective the forces of nature are both unpredictable and uncontrollable (v. 3). Human beings do not know what good or bad things "may happen on earth" (v. 2), just as they do not know how a baby becomes alive in the womb. Once again, as in 3:11 and 8:17, Qohelet declares that the work of God cannot be fully known to humankind.

However, Qohelet does not think that our inescapable ignorance about the future is a valid reason for inaction. If you wait until you think you know what is going to happen, he says, you will never get anything done (11:4). Instead, you need to go ahead and do whatever needs to be done, realizing that "you do not know" which of the things you do will have positive results and which will not (v. 6).

Qohelet's advice implicitly contradicts the majority of opinions represented in Proverbs (e.g., Prov. 12:21; 13:21; 13:16). But even the proverbially wise occasionally recognized the uncertainty of the future: "Do not boast about tomorrow, for you do not know what a day may bring forth" (Prov. 27:1). Qohelet counsels us to act

190

boldly and to take risks, being fully aware that there are no guarantees that "wise" deeds will prosper or that foolish endeavors will fail. In the final analysis we have no security other than the grace of God.

LIFE IS FLEETING AND SWEET (11:7-8)

Only one thing, in Qohelet's opinion, is certain. Everything that happens under the sun is *hebel,* a breath. All of Qohelet's observations and deliberations have led him to the same conclusion: life is a swiftly passing sweetness which ought to be savored and enjoyed for the brief moment it lasts. In Qohelet's opinion it is important for us to remember that the "days of darkness will be many." Such a reminder ought not to dampen our pleasure in the light. Instead, Qohelet seems to argue that an acute sense of life's brevity should increase the degree to which we cherish life while we have it (Eccl. 11:7-8). The same thing will be said about youth in 11:9–12:1.

THE DAWN OF LIFE IS BRIEF (11:9-10)

Eccl. 11:9-10 continues the thoughts begun in vv. 7-8 and acts as an introduction to Qohelet's concluding remarks in 12:1-7. Just as the brevity of life increases the intensity with which we enjoy it, so the days of our youth (which pass so swiftly) should also be the source of intense joy. Qohelet advises young people to turn aside the sorrows of their minds and the troubles of their bodies (11:10). Youth, like the blackness of dawn, is *hebel* (swiftly vanishing) and thus should not be wasted. Young people should "rejoice" in their youth. They should do whatever their hearts and their minds desire—without forgetting, however, that God will eventually "judge" them for what they do (v. 9). Some readers have suggested that this reference to God's "judgment" is out of place here. But it seems to me that 3:12-22 and 8:12-15 make essentially the same point. In all three passages Qohelet affirms, on the one hand, that God wants us to enjoy the good things in life while, on the other hand, continuing to uphold the idea that God will (eventually) evaluate how well we have used our time "under the sun." Qohelet does not banish accountability from his system of values. He simply denies that accountability takes a material form "under the sun."

191

CHAPTER TWELVE

The chapter begins with Qohelet's final speech (12:1-7). Qohelet's own words end with v. 7, and in v. 8 the thematic statement "all is *hebel*" (with which the book began) is repeated. Again (as in 1:2) the thematic statement is phrased as a third person comment *about* Qohelet rather than *by* him. The conclusion to the book of Ecclesiastes consists of an editorial summary of Qohelet's work (12:9-10) and some comments on the nature and the value of the "words of the wise" collection as a whole (vv. 11-14).

THE DUSK OF LIFE (12:1-8)

The advice which Qohelet directed to an unnamed youth in 11:9 continues in 12:1-7. The first verse picks up the theme of "remembering" from 11:8. "Remember also your Creator in the days of your youth" is a correct and traditional rendering of the Hebrew text as it now stands. However, another Hebrew word which is pronounced the same as the word for Creator (but is spelled slightly differently) means "grave," and many interpreters suggest that "Remember your grave in the days of your youth" is more likely to represent the speaker's intentions. Since the passage ends with words which call to mind the Creation narrative in Gen. 2–3, the translation "Creator" seems to me to be adequate for Qohelet's purposes. "Remembering" means more in its OT usages than merely bringing something to mind. Those who are asked to "remember" their "Creator" are being called to judge their actions in light of what they know (or think they know) about God.

Beginning with the last two verses of the previous chapter, the listener is advised to remember that "youth and the dawn of life" are gone as quickly as a breath (Eccl. 11:10) and that the years which swiftly draw near will hold less intense pleasure (12:1) and

192

You are looking at your future

will inevitably end in death (v. 7). All of the phrases from the middle of v. 1 to the end of v. 7 are a part of the same sense unit, which says in effect, "while you are still young, remember that the following things will soon apply to you." If 12:1-7 is read as a part of a unit beginning with 11:9, it becomes a call to live both joyfully and responsibly during "youth and the dawn of life."

Most interpreters have read 12:2-5 as a series of metaphors describing the decreasing physical vitality which often comes with old age, leading to death (poetically described in v. 6) and to the consequences of death (v. 7). A few interpreters have seen the description of a decaying house or estate lying beneath the surface of the text, while others suggest that the picture which vv. 3-5 evoke is that of a community in mourning (at the time of a funeral) showing signs of respect towards the deceased (see Michael V. Fox, *Qohelet and His Contradictions,* 280-298). But by far the majority of readers see more specific and personal references to muscular tremors, gnarled limbs, scarcity of teeth, and failing eyesight in v. 3 and descriptions of hearing or speaking disorders (and some would say a reference to the tendency of the elderly to wake up early) in v. 4. The Egyptian vizier Ptah-hotep describes old age with a similar mix of metaphorical and literal language (cf. *ANET,* 412).

Most readers are ready to agree that the "grinders" and "those that look through the windows" (Eccl. 12:3) are fairly clear figures for teeth (which grow few) and eyes (which grow dim), and that the "keepers of the house" and the "strong men" probably refer to arms and legs, though not everyone agrees on which is which. However, there is very little agreement concerning the meaning of the images in vv. 4-5. Some interpreters think that the first two phrases in v. 5 refer to the heightened risks and increased difficulties older people face in getting from place to place, but the metaphor of the grasshopper is quite unclear. The white blossoms of the almond tree call forth an image of a head of white hair, but the meaning of the phrase which the RSV has translated "desire fails" is very uncertain.

It is not really necessary to find a one-to-one equivalence between the original language of this text and the potential infirmities of old age in order to understand that Qohelet is here describing the "dusk" (in contrast to the dawn) of life. The ambiguity of the imagery contributes to rather than detracts from the effectiveness of the passage. Rather than spelling out the specifics of the process of aging, the metaphors evoke an atmosphere of decline and decay, leading towards the finality of death. Thus, different individuals may find their own experiences or observations concerning aging and death reflected in different facets of the language. In whatever way the metaphors are explained, the whole adds up to a portrait of a person who is headed towards his or her "eternal home."

In 11:7 Qohelet used "light" and one's ability to see the sun as metaphors for life and its natural pleasures, in contrast to the coming "days of darkness" (v. 8). In 12:2 the image of gathering gloom sets the stage for the coming of death, which is preceded by the twilight of life.

The metaphors in v. 6 are euphemisms for death itself. When the cord from which a lamp is hanging snaps, the "golden bowl" of the lamp is shattered. When the rope pulley by which a water jar is lowered into a well breaks, the jar is also broken. And when the tenuous thread of a person's life is broken, the dust of which he or she is made returns to the earth and the spirit [breath] returns to the Creator (v. 7). Again, as in 3:20 the words "dust" and "return" echo those used at the end of the story of "Eden" [which means "pleasure"] (Gen. 3:19).

In the United States the onset of old age and the coming of death are seldom discussed openly. The infirmities which often accompany the "dusk" of life are considered embarrassing or shameful. We hide (and hide from) the realities of life, rather than "remembering" them as Qohelet advises. Qohelet's attitude towards old age resembles the modern counseling technique known as reality therapy. Honesty can often be therapeutic. Boldly facing the difficult realities in life enables us to confront and to manage our fear of them.

The children who make the least fuss about getting an inoculation are the ones who are told (1) that the procedure will hurt a bit and (2) that they are capable of handling the pain. The ones who have been told "It won't hurt a bit" have a hard time coping with both their discomfort and their sense of having been betrayed. In a similar way, Qohelet advises the not-yet-old that their years of diminished strength draw nigh and that they will be wise to keep this reality in mind.

Qohelet's "reality therapy" consists of an honest look at the potential pain of getting old and of dying, combined with a final

194

reassurance. Although the words used are not identical, the comfort Qohelet offers also is reminiscent of the Creation story in Gen. 2–3. Just as God originally formed us from the dust of the ground and breathed into our nostrils the breath of life so that we became living beings (Gen. 2:7), says Qohelet, so when we die, "the dust returns to the earth as it was, and the spirit [breath] returns to God who gave it" (Eccl. 12:7).

The third person statement of the theme which characterizes Qohelet's work (v. 8) acts as conclusion both to the poem on the dusk of life and to the collected sayings of Qohelet. If, as we have assumed throughout this commentary, the word *hebel* refers to that which is transitory, then the addition of v. 8 to the description of aging and death may also be taken as a word of comfort. These things too last only as long as a puff of wind in the overall plan of God.

A SUMMARY OF QOHELET'S CAREER (12:9-10)

Qohelet was remembered as one who shared his wisdom. He did not merely hoard his knowledge; he also taught it to others. Part of his work involved "weighing and studying and arranging proverbs with great care." In other words Qohelet was known for his ability to test the soundness of traditional sayings (to "weigh" them) and to put them in their proper contexts (to "arrange" them). The RSV links the two statements in v. 10 with "and," giving the reader the impression that Qohelet gave about the same amount of weight to finding "pleasing words" as he did to writing "words of truth." However, the conjunction in Hebrew can be translated "but" as well as "and." I suggest that this comment on Qohelet's motives implies that he valued truth higher than "pleasing words." The person who summarized Qohelet's career believed that Qohelet always tried to find pleasing words for what he had to say, *but* "uprightly he wrote words of truth" (even if he could not find a pleasant way to express what needed to be said).

THE SAYINGS OF THE WISE ARE LIKE GOADS (12:11-14)

The phrase "sayings of the wise" in v. 11 is the same in Hebrew as "the words of the wise" in Prov. 1:6; 22:17; 24:23, and the translation "like goads" (meaning some type of tool with a sharp edge or point) is fairly certain. But the meaning of the Hebrew in the second half of Eccl. 12:11 is very uncertain. There seems to be an attempt to compare the task of collecting the sayings of the wise with the actions of a shepherd prodding and gathering a flock into some sort of order. The capitalization of "Shepherd" may be misleading to modern readers. Hebrew does not have capital letter forms. The translators who put capitals into the English text make what seems to be a generic noun in Hebrew into a proper noun in English. The emphasis in the Hebrew seems to be on the purpose for which the collection was made rather than on the person who "rounded up" the scattered sayings of the wise ones of Israel.

The advice which begins with "My son" in v. 12 is reminiscent of the Instructions in Prov. 1–9. If the prologue to Proverbs (Prov. 1:1-7) and the epilogue to Ecclesiastes (Eccl. 12:11ff.) can be attributed to the same editor(s), as we have assumed throughout this commentary, then "beyond these" in v. 12 must refer to the whole collection, including both Proverbs and Ecclesiastes. The speaker thinks that what has been gathered together in these two books is an adequate basis for the "son's" wisdom education. The "son" is thus advised not to look for anything further (in terms of wisdom) than these. In its present setting, the last sentence in v. 12 gives a rationale for this advice. But authors and students today can appreciate the truth of this saying as a generalization (taken out of its context). Truly, "of making many books there is no end, and much study is a weariness of the flesh"!

This, says the final editor or commentator in v. 13, is the "end of the matter." Enough has now been heard. Anyone reading the collected sayings of the wise should now be able to conclude that the wholeness (RSV "whole duty") of humankind is based on reverence for God.

The last piece of advice given in Ecclesiastes ("Fear God, and keep his commandments. . . . For God will bring every deed into judgment. . . .") has often been understood by modern interpreters as a negation of Qohelet's sayings or as a warning that the pious should not be goaded by the words of the wise into forgetting the essence of their faith. But this advice does not seem to me to be a contradiction of what Qohelet has said. Qohelet does not advocate any form of action contrary to the "commandments." And in his meditations he frequently commends the attitude of respectful awe known as the "fear of God." But, unlike the writers of Proverbs, who confidently assert that "the reward for humility and fear of the LORD is riches and honor and life" (Prov. 22:4), Qohelet suggests that those who keep the commandments cannot count on receiving their "just deserts" in their lives "under the sun."

Qohelet's insistence that we humans cannot know anything substantial about God's plans or about God's works represents a genuinely respectful attitude towards God. The speakers in Proverbs seem confident of their ability to predict how God will deal with either the wicked or the righteous. But Qohelet is much more humble. When he affirms that God will eventually bring every deed into judgment (as in Eccl. 11:9), he resists the urge to identify what the results of God's deliberations will be. Thus, the editorial comment which brings the collected words of the wise to a close acts as a confirmation rather than as a denial of Qohelet's thinking. Both Qohelet and the editor are willing to leave such things as rewards and punishments up to God's discretion.

THE ROLE OF ECCLESIASTES
IN THE CANON

Eugene H. Peterson says that Ecclesiastes "functions not as a meal but as a bath. It is not nourishment; it is cleansing" (*Five Smooth Stones for Pastoral Work*, 125). Qohelet throws a splash of cold water in the faces of those who are tempted to think that they have discovered all the answers. He depresses the pretensions of those who think they can guarantee themselves happiness through their own endeavors. He confronts the complacent with the fragility of those things upon which they have leaned so heavily, and he goads the prosperous into reconsidering the sources of their prosperity.

While we cannot locate a precise historical setting for Qohelet or his original audience, we can see that he challenges the retributive expectations which surface in so many parts of the book of Proverbs. We can also see that Qohelet counters and denies the universal validity of many of the observations made by the wise who contributed to Proverbs. On the one hand, Qohelet reminds his audiences of the limited nature of proverbial truths by appealing to his own contrary experiences "under the sun." On the other hand, his continual references to what can be said to be true "under the sun" function as subtle suggestions that "under the sun" may not be all there is.

In the liturgical tradition of Judaism, the book of Ecclesiastes is read as a part of the religious observance of Sukkot (the Feast of Booths or Tabernacles). Sukkot (which Jesus is said to have participated in; John 7:1-39) is a feast of joy, celebrated at the close of the harvest season (Deut. 16:13-15). It is a time set aside to give thanks to God for the abundance which the community has gathered in from the land. But by tradition it is also a time to remember when there were no crops and no harvest, when the people of God wandered in the wilderness, living in flimsy and temporary shelters *(sukkot)*. At the very time when the people of

198

Israel celebrated the bounty of the cultivated land, they were commanded to remember the days when they had no crops to harvest—the time when they depended on God alone for sustenance of life (Lev. 23:33-44).

It is at this festival of thanksgiving and joy that the words of Qohelet are read as a reminder to those who are in the midst of their abundance that all of these material blessings are fleeting—they are as transitory as a breath of wind. Like life, they are gifts of God to be used and enjoyed but not hoarded.

This liturgical tradition can give both Christians and Jews further insight into the function Ecclesiastes serves as a part of our canon of sacred Scriptures. Whether you celebrate Sukkot or not, whether you rejoice in a good harvest or a good business year or a good school year (or even if you are merely glad to have survived another year)—whenever you count your "blessings"—reading the words of Qohelet will help you remember that your possessions, your wisdom, your loved ones, your youth, your health, and your life are all transitory. They are *hebel,* a "breath"—lacking in permanence but not in worth.

And if, in counting your blessings, you are tempted to think that you have received them as a reward for your righteousness, reading Ecclesiastes might help convince you that there is no correspondence "under the sun" between your faithfulness and the possessions you accumulate.

THE FUNCTION
OF THE COLLECTED WORDS
OF THE WISE

Neither Proverbs nor Ecclesiastes taken alone presents the reader with a large enough glimpse of the reality of God to fill the needs of a faith in search of understanding. But the editorial joining of the two books within the context of the canon (see the previous discussion of their present arrangement on p. 4) goes a long way towards providing our communities of faith with sustenance for the continuing journey. The wise whose words have been gathered into the canon were all hoping to discover "what is good for humankind to do." But the contributors to Proverbs and Ecclesiastes came to a number of different (and sometimes contradictory) conclusions. Those who preserved and handed these materials on to us did not simply accept one set of answers and reject the rest. They deliberately retained the whole, complete with its variety. They put an "end to the matter" (Eccl. 12:13) before anyone could offer a definitive answer to the question of how those who are both wise and faithful should live out their lives under the sun. Thus the collectors themselves compel us to engage in a continuing conversation with the wise. "All streams run to the sea, but the sea is not full" (1:7). Nor is our hunger to know what is good for us to do in our brief lives under the sun ever satisfied. We are called upon to live out our lives in risk, trusting in nothing less than the enduring grace of God.

APPENDIX

THE PLACE OF ECCLESIASTES
IN THE DEVELOPMENT
OF BIBLICAL IDEAS
ABOUT LIFE AFTER DEATH

Most scholars agree that the Hebrew Scriptures contain few, if any, clear references to the concept of an afterlife. In a recent and extremely thorough examination of the evidence, Klaas Spronk concludes that the OT is remarkably reticent to speak about any hope for the individual after death other than "the trust that the communion of the faithful with God shall last forever" (*Beatific Afterlife in Ancient Israel and in the Ancient Near East*, 345). In most OT texts Yahweh is pictured primarily as a god of the living. Only a few verses can be found which might illustrate the hope that Yahweh's faithfulness *(hesed)* towards the faithful will continue after death (e.g., Ps. 73, 49, 16). Other than Dan. 12:2 (and some would add Isa. 26:19), the OT texts contain nothing but ambiguous hints or obscure clues to whatever popular beliefs were held by individual Israelites. Spronk attributes this "reluctance to speak about help of YHWH after death" not to lack of interest in the matter but to "the fear of becoming entangled in the Canaanite religious ideas about life and death" (344).

However, sometime between the end of the OT period and the beginning of the NT period, this reticence on the part of the Jewish community seems to have come to an end. A number of NT texts refer to what appear to be rather well-known and well-developed ideas (among the audiences to which they were addressed) concerning judgments and rewards for individuals taking place after their deaths. Scholarly discussions usually attribute such conceptual developments to outside influences, such as contacts between Jewish and Persian or Greek communities.

In the OT the word *sheol* is sometimes used to refer to a shadowy underworld, an abode of the dead (e.g., Prov. 9:18), which is pictured as being located in the bowels of the earth (Prov. 15:24). On other occasions Sheol is used merely as a synonym for death.

Sometimes Sheol is pictured as a realm of silence and forgetfulness (e.g., Job 7:7-10). Qohelet seems to have been inclined towards this understanding (cf. Eccl. 9:5, 10). But in other OT passages the dead are credited with powers of speech and are said to retain the status they had when alive (e.g., Isa. 14:9-20; Ezek. 32:18-32). Sometimes the realm of the dead is thought to be removed from Yahweh's vicinity or jurisdiction (cf. Ps. 88:3-5, 10-12; Isa. 38:18), while other texts affirm an opposite understanding (e.g., Ps. 139:7-8). Occasionally, *Sheol* is personified as an active power, as though it had some mythological life of its own (e.g., Isa. 5:14). (See Spronk, 66-70.)

The KJV translates about half of the OT uses of *sheol* with the English word "hell" and the other half by the word "grave." However, in English "hell" is usually taken to be a reference to a place of punishment after death, while nearly all OT references to Sheol portray it as a destination to which all the dead go, regardless of whether their lives were lived in righteous or in wicked ways. Since the word which is often translated "soul" *(nephesh)* refers to a whole person (as in the English usage "I didn't see a soul that I knew"), statements such as "thou hast delivered my soul from the depths of Sheol" (Ps. 86:13) are understood by most interpreters to refer to escape from death itself rather than escape from punishment after death.

Scholars commonly agree that the majority of OT witnesses expected retribution (i.e., rewards and punishments for good and bad behavior) to occur "under the sun." In some texts an individual's sin is said to bring punishment upon an entire community (Josh. 7). In others retribution is expected to extend into the future, affecting the descendants of those who show "love" or "hate" towards God (e.g., Exod. 20:5-6 and its many parallels). However, Jer. 31:29-30; Ezek. 18:1-20 clearly deny the traditions of communal or inherited responsibility and assert that "the righteousness of the righteous shall be upon himself, and the wickedness of the wicked shall be upon himself" (Ezek. 18:20b).

Many members of the Israelite community of faith clearly expected to receive tangible, material rewards for their behavior (e.g., Deut. 7:12–8:20; Prov. 2:21-22; 10:2-3). However, such retributive theologies must have needed continual reinforcement from experience to survive. The speaker in Ps. 58 asks God to provide "the righteous" with visible proof that "there is a God who judges on earth" (v. 11). Clearly, it becomes a problem for the believer if such evidence is not forthcoming. Ps. 37 seems to be addressed to those who question retribution theology, and Ps. 73 contains the confessions of one who was tempted to do so ("I was envious of the arrogant, when I saw the prosperity of the wicked"; v. 3) but who resisted temptation by concluding that the wicked will eventually perish (v. 27), implying (though not actually saying) that the righteous will not.

Within the Wisdom tradition both Job and Qohelet challenge their audiences to weigh the evidence of their eyes and ears over against the traditional doctrine of retribution. Thus, Job asks his listeners to compare the proverbial assertion that "the lamp of the wicked will be put out" (Prov. 13:9) with their own life experience: "How often is it that the lamp of the wicked is put out? That their calamity comes upon them?" (Job 21:17), and with others' experiences: "Have you not asked those who travel the roads, and do you not accept their testimony that the wicked man is spared in the day of calamity, that he is rescued in the day of wrath?" (Job 21:29-30).

Qohelet tells us that he, too, has paid careful attention to the world around him. And even during his own brief lifetime he has seen "a righteous man who perishes in his righteousness" and "a wicked man who prolongs his life in his evil-doing" (Eccl. 7:15). When one observes life carefully, one cannot help but notice that there are indeed "righteous" people "to whom it happens according to the deeds of the wicked" and that there are "wicked" people "to whom it happens according to the deeds of the righteous" (8:14; cf. v. 10). Thus, on the basis of his own experience, Qohelet concludes that "under the sun the race is not [necessarily] to the swift, nor the battle to the strong, nor bread to the wise, nor riches to the intelligent, nor favor to the men of skill" (9:11). It is in fact the case, "under the sun," that "one fate comes to all," whether they are foolish or wise, righteous or wicked, good or evil, human or animal (9:2-3; 2:14; 3:19). All living beings "go to one place; all are from the dust, and all turn to dust again" (3:20).

However, Qohelet does not deny the possibility that God's judgment might take place somewhere outside of human experience. In fact there are several passages in Ecclesiastes which hint at such a belief: "Though a sinner does evil a hundred times and prolongs his life, yet I know that it will be well with those who fear

God, because they fear before him; but it will not be well with the wicked . . ." (8:12-13; cf. 11:9; 3:17).

Critics of the consistency of Qohelet's viewpoint have suggested that such hints were added by "pious editors" or glossators who adhered to the traditional retributive viewpoint. But these editorial theories do nothing to explain the frequency with which Qohelet uses such phrases as "under the sun," "on earth," and "under the sky." These expressions seem to me to imply that the speaker thinks a distinction can be made between what happens in human experience (under the sun) and what happens elsewhere. Thus, I would suggest that both Qohelet and his audience share an interest in the question of the existence of some form of afterlife. Once convinced that the traditional doctrine of retribution fails to reflect human experience, one either has to give up the idea of justice or one has to push its execution into some realm beyond the evidence of human experience. However, Qohelet shares the reticence of most other OT witnesses on the subject of what such an afterlife might look like. He insists that we human beings cannot know for sure "what comes after" our brief life "under the sun" (3:21; 6:12; 7:14). But having argued that there is an appropriate time for everything "under heaven" (in 3:1-8), he finds it appropriate to conclude that he also can trust God to "appoint" a time to "judge the righteous and the wicked" (3:17).

SELECTED BIBLIOGRAPHY

Books

Aitken, Kenneth T. *Proverbs.* The Daily Study Bible (Philadelphia: Westminster and Edinburgh: Saint Andrews, 1986).

Barton, George A. *Ecclesiastes.* International Critical Commentary (1908; repr. Edinburgh: T. & T. Clark, 1908).

Barton, John. *Reading the Old Testament: Method in Biblical Study* (Philadelphia: Westminster and London: Darton, Longman & Todd, 1984).

Bergant, Dianne. *Job, Ecclesiastes.* Old Testament Message 18 (Wilmington: Michael Glazier, 1982).

Brueggemann, Walter. *In Man We Trust: The Neglected Side of Biblical Faith* (Richmond: John Knox, 1972).

Camp, Claudia V. *Wisdom and the Feminine in the Book of Proverbs.* Bible and Literature Series 11 (Sheffield: Almond, 1985).

Collins, John J. *Proverbs, Ecclesiastes.* Knox Preaching Guides (Atlanta: John Knox, 1980).

Cowley, A. E. *Aramaic Papyri of the Fifth Century B.C.* (1923; repr. Osnabrück: Zeller, 1976).

Cox, Dermot. *Proverbs, with an Introduction to Sapiential Books.* Old Testament Message 17 (Wilmington: Michael Glazier, 1982).

Crenshaw, James L. *Ecclesiastes.* Old Testament Library (Philadelphia: Westminster and London: SCM, 1987).

_____. *Old Testament Wisdom: An Introduction* (Atlanta: John Knox, 1981).

_____. ed. *Studies in Ancient Israelite Wisdom* (New York: KTAV, 1976).

Davidson, Robert. *The Courage to Doubt: Exploring an Old Testament Theme* (London: SCM Press, 1983).

_____. *Ecclesiastes and Song of Solomon.* The Daily Study Bible (Philadelphia: Westminster and Edinburgh: Saint Andrews, 1986).

Derousseaux, Louis. *La crainte de Dieu dans l'Ancien Testament.* Lectio divina 63 (Paris: Les Editions du Cerf, 1970).

Ellermeier, Friedrich. *Qohelet,* 2 vol. (Herzberg: Erwin Jungfer, 1967-1970).

Fox, Michael V. *Qohelet and His Contradictions.* Bible and Literature Series 18 (Sheffield: Almond Press, 1989).

Fredericks, Daniel C. *Qoheleth's Language: Re-evaluating Its Nature and Date.* Ancient Near Eastern Texts and Studies 3 (Lewiston, N.Y.: Edwin Mellen, 1988).

Ginsburg, Christian D. *The Song of Songs and Coheleth* (1857-1861; repr. New York: KTAV, 1970).

Gordis, Robert. *Koheleth—The Man and His World,* 3rd ed. (New York: Shoceken, 1968).

Greenstone, Julius H. *Proverbs.* The Holy Scriptures with Commentary (Philadelphia: Jewish Publication Society of America, 1950).

Isaksson, Bo. *Studies in the Language of Qoheleth.* Studia Semitica Upsaliensia 10 (Uppsala: Acta Universitatis Upsaliensis, 1987).

Kidner, Derek. *The Wisdom of Proverbs, Job and Ecclesiastes* (Downers Grove and Leicester: InterVarsity, 1985).

Kushner, Harold S. *When All You've Ever Wanted Isn't Enough* (New York: Summit, 1986).

Lang, Bernhard. *Wisdom and the Book of Proverbs* (New York: Pilgrim, 1986).

Leiman, Sid Z. *The Canonization of Hebrew Scripture: The Talmudic and Midrashic Evidence.* Transactions of the Connecticut Academy of Arts and Sciences 47 (Hamden, Conn.: Archon, 1976).

McKane, William. *Proverbs: A New Approach.* Old Testament Library (Philadelphia: Westminster and London: SCM, 1970).

Murphy, Roland E. *Wisdom Literature.* Forms of the Old Testament Literature 13 (Grand Rapids: Wm. B. Eerdmans, 1981).

Nare, Laurent. *Proverbes salomoniens et proverbes mossi: Étude com-*

parative à partir d'une nouvelle analyse de Pr 25–29. Europäische Hochschulschriften 23/283 (Frankfort-am-Main: Peter Lang, 1986).

Nickelsburg, George W. E., and Stone, Michael E. *Faith and Piety in Early Judaism: Texts and Documents* (Philadelphia: Fortress, 1983).

Ogden, Graham S. *Qoheleth* (Sheffield: JSOT Press, 1987).

Peterson, Eugene H. *Five Smooth Stones for Pastoral Work* (Atlanta: John Knox, 1980).

von Rad, Gerhard. *Wisdom in Israel* (Nashville: Abingdon and London: SCM, 1972).

Scott, R. B. Y. *Proverbs–Ecclesiastes.* Anchor Bible 18 (Garden City: Doubleday, 1965).

_____. *The Way of Wisdom in the Old Testament* (New York: Macmillan, 1971).

Spronk, Klaus. *Beatific Afterlife in Ancient Israel and in the Ancient Near East* (Kevelaer: Butzon und Bercker and Neukirchen-Vluyn: Neukirchener, 1986).

Thompson, John M. *The Form and Function of Proverbs in Ancient Israel.* Studia Judaica 1 (The Hague: Mouton, 1974).

Toy, Crawford H. *Proverbs.* International Critical Commentary (1899; repr. Edinburgh: T. & T. Clark, 1970).

Whitley, Charles F. *Koheleth: His Language and Thought.* Beihefte zur Zeitschrift für die alttestamentliche Wissenschaft 148 (Berlin and New York: Walter de Gruyter, 1979).

Whybray, Roger N. *The Book of Proverbs.* Cambridge Bible Commentary (Cambridge: Cambridge University Press, 1972).

_____. *Wisdom in Proverbs.* Studies in Biblical Theology 45 (London: SCM and Naperville: Allenson, 1965).

Wilson, Marvin R. *Our Father Abraham: Jewish Roots of the Christian Faith* (Grand Rapids: Wm. B. Eerdmans and Dayton: Center for Judaic-Christian Studies, 1989).

Articles

Allegro, John M. " 'The Wiles of the Wicked Woman': A Sapiential Work from Qumran's Fourth Cave," *Palestine Exploration Quarterly* 96 (1964): 53-55.

Bream, Howard N. "Life without Resurrection: Two Perspectives from Qoheleth," in *A Light Unto My Path: Old Testament*

Studies in Honor of Jacob M. Myers, ed. Howard N. Bream, Ralph D. Heim, and Carey A. Moore (Philadelphia: Temple University Press, 1974), 49-65.

Bryce, Glendon E. "'Better'—Proverbs: An Historical and Structural Study," *Society of Biblical Literature 1972 Proceedings* 2:343-354.

_____. "Another Wisdom-'Book' in Proverbs," *Journal of Biblical Literature* 91 (1972): 145-157.

Chopineau, Jacques. "Une image de l'homme: Sur Ecclesiaste 1,2," *Études théologiques et religieuses* 53 (1978): 366-370.

Collins, John J. "Proverbial Wisdom and the Yahwist Vision," *Semeia* 17 (1980): 1-17.

Crüsemann, Frank. "The Unchangeable World: The 'Crisis of Wisdom' in Koheleth," in *God of the Lowly: Socio-Historical Interpretations of the Bible,* ed. Willy Schottroff and Wolfgang Stegemann (Maryknoll: Orbis, 1984), 57-77.

Dahood, Mitchell. "Immortality in Proverbs 12, 28," *Biblica* 41 (1960): 176-181.

DeVries, Carl E. "The Bearing of Current Egyptian Studies on the Old Testament," in *New Perspectives on the Old Testament,* ed. J. Barton Payne. (Waco: Word, 1970), 25-36.

Fensham, F. Charles. "Widow, Orphan and the Poor in Ancient Near Eastern Legal and Wisdom Literature," *Journal of Near Eastern Studies* 21 (1962): 129-139.

Fox, Michael V. "Aging and Death in Qohelet 12," *Journal for the Study of the Old Testament* 42 (1988): 55-77.

_____. "Frame-Narrative and Composition in the Book of Qohelet," *Hebrew Union College Annual* 48 (1977): 83-106.

_____. "The Meaning of *Hebel* for Qohelet," *Journal of Biblical Literature* 105 (1986): 409-427.

Garrett, Duane A. "Qohelet on the Use and Abuse of Political Power," *Trinity Journal* 8 (1987): 159-177.

Good, Edwin M. J. "The Unfilled Sea: Style and Meaning in Ecclesiastes 1:2-11," in *Israelite Wisdom: Theological and Literary Essays in Honor of Samuel Terrien,* ed. John G. Gammie et al. (Missoula: Scholars Press, 1978), 59-73.

Gowan, Donald E. "Wealth and Poverty in the Old Testament: The Case of the Widow, the Orphan, and the Sojourner," *Interpretation* 41 (1987): 341-367.

Habel, Norman C. "Symbolism of Wisdom in Proverbs 1–9," *Interpretation* 26 (1972): 131-157.

Helmbold, Andrew K. "The Relationship of Proverbs and Amenemope," in *Law and the Prophets: Old Testament Studies Prepared in Honor of Oswald Thompson Allis,* ed. John H. Skilton (Nutley, N.J.: Presbyterian and Reformed, 1974), 348-359.

Hildebrandt, Ted. "Proverbial Pairs: Compositional Units in Proverbs 10–29," *Journal of Biblical Literature* 107 (1988): 207-224.

Holm-Nielsen, Svend. "The Book of Ecclesiastes and the Interpretation of It in Jewish and Christian Theology," *Annual of the Swedish Theological Institute* 10 (1975-1976): 38-96.

Johnston, Robert K. "'Confessions of a Workaholic': A Reappraisal of Qoheleth," *Catholic Biblical Quarterly* 38 (1976): 14-28.

Kugel, James L. "Qohelet and Money," *Catholic Biblical Quarterly* 51 (1989): 32-49.

Landes, George M. "Creation Tradition in Proverbs 8:22-31 and Genesis 1," in *A Light Unto My Path,* 279-293.

Loader, J. A. "Qohelet 3_{2-8}: A 'Sonnet' in the Old Testament," *Zeitschrift für die alttestamentliche Wissenschaft* 81 (1969): 240-42.

Lys, Daniel. "L'Être et le temps: Communication de Qohèlèth," in *La Sagesse de l'Ancien Testament,* ed. M. Gilbert. Bibliotheca Ephemeridum Theologicarum Louvaniensium 51 (Leuven: University Press and Gembloux: Duculot, 1979), 249-258.

McCreesh, Thomas P. "Wisdom as Wife: Proverbs 31:10-31," *Revue biblique* 92 (1985): 25-46.

Muilenburg, James. "A Qoheleth Scroll from Qumran," *Bulletin of the American Schools of Oriental Research* 135 (1954): 20-28.

Murphy, Roland E. "Qoheleth's 'Quarrel' with the Fathers," in *From Faith to Faith: Essays in Honor of Donald G. Miller on His Seventieth Birthday.* ed. Dikran Y. Hadidian. Pittsburgh Theological Monographs 31 (Pittsburgh: Pickwick, 1979), 235-245.

_____. "Qohelet Interpreted: The Bearing of the Past on the Present," *Vetus Testamentum* 32 (1982): 331-37.

_____. "Wisdom and Creation," *Journal of Biblical Literature* 104 (1985): 3-11.

Ogden, Graham S. ʿQoheleth XI 7–XII 8: Qoheleth's Summons to Enjoyment and Reflection," *Vetus Testamentum* 34 (1984): 27-38.

_____. "Qoheleth's Use of the 'Nothing is Better' Form," *Journal of Biblical Literature* 98 (1979): 339-350.

Priest, John F. "Humanism, Skepticism, and Pessimism in Israel," *Journal of the American Academy of Religion* 36 (1968): 311-326.

Roth, Wolfgang M. W. "The Numerical Sequence x/x+1 in the Old Testament," *Vetus Testamentum* 12 (1962): 300-311.

Sanders, James. "Biblical Criticism and the Bible as Canon," *Union Seminary Quarterly Review* 32 (1977): 157-165.

Sawyer, John F. A. "The Ruined House in Ecclesiastes 12: A Reconstruction of the Original Parable," *Journal of Biblical Literature* 94 (1975): 519-531.

Scott, R. B. Y. "Wise and Foolish, Righteous and Wicked: Literary Criticism of Proverbs," in *Studies in the Religion of Ancient Israel.* Supplements to Vetus Testamentum 23 (1972): 146-165.

Shupak, Nil. "The 'Sitz im Leben' of the Book of Proverbs in the Light of a Comparison of Biblical and Egyptian Wisdom Literature," *Revue biblique* 94 (1987): 98-119.

Skehan, Patrick W. "Wisdom's House," *Catholic Biblical Quarterly* 29 (1967): 468-86.

Spina, Frank Anthony. "Qoheleth and the Reformation of Wisdom," in *The Quest for the Kingdom of God: Studies in Honor of George E. Mendenhall,* ed. Herbert B. Huffmon, Frank Anthony Spina, and Alberto R. W. Green (Winona Lake: Eisenbrauns, 1983), 267-279.

Terrien, Samuel. "The Play of Wisdom: Turning Point in Biblical Theology," *Horizons in Biblical Theology* 3 (1981): 125-153.

Vawter, Bruce. "Intimations of Immortality and the Old Testament," *Journal of Biblical Literature* 91 (1972): 158-171.

_____. "Prov 8:22: Wisdom and Creation," *Journal of Biblical Literature* 99 (1980): 205-216.

Walsh, Jerome. "Despair as a Theological Virtue in the Spirituality of Ecclesiastes," *Biblical Theological Bulletin* 12 (1982): 46-49.

Whybray, Roger N. "The Identification and Use of Quotations in Ecclesiastes," *Supplements to Vetus Testamentum* 32 (1980): 435-451.

_____. "Qoheleth Preacher of Joy," *Journal for the Study of the Old Testement* 23 (1982): 87-98.

Wilson, Gerald H. "'The Words of the Wise': The Intent and Significance of Qohelet 12:9-14," *Journal of Biblical Literature* 103 (1984): 175-192.

Wolters, Al. "Ṣôpiyyâ (Prov 31:27) as Hymnic Participle and Play on *Sophia*," Journal of Biblical Literature 104 (1985): 577-587.

Wright, Addison G. "The Riddle of the Sphinx: The Structure of the Book of Qoheleth," *Catholic Biblical Quarterly* 30 (1968): 313-334.

INDEX OF
SCRIPTURE REFERENCES

Printed in the United States
69668LV00002B/191